His Beloved

Renew. Transform. Prosper. Devotional

Geneva Jewel

Copyright © 2017 by Geneva Jewel LLC
All rights reserved.
This book or any portion thereof may not be reproduced or used in any manner whatsoever without the express written permission of the publisher
except for the use of brief quotations in a book review.

Printed in the United States of America
First Printing, 2017
ISBN 978-0-9989803-1-7 (Paperback)

School of Kingdom Identity
Bear, DE

www.GenevaJewel.com

Dedication

This devotional could be dedicated to a lot of people, but I want to dedicate it to the person that is reading it right now! I honestly wrote it for you. I had been hurting for so long and I just wanted to share how God's word (The Bible) helped me move out of that place of being stuck. This is for the person who battles with their mindset on a daily basis and the only thing you want is peace. I wrote it for you. This is for the woman who wants to love God whole heartedly but condemnation is your best friend. This is for anyone who is ready to walk in your true Kingdom Identity. It's time to ready our hearts and fill our minds with what and who God says that we are. No more walking around defeated. The battle has already been won and you can walk in victory!!

This devotional is dedicated to the VICTORIUS!! That is my prophesy over You!!

Special Thanks!

I thank my inner circle. I have too many to name so if I don't please don't hold it against me. My husband, Garth, I thank you for coming into my life and pushing me to complete this project. You were prayed for before we even met and God has exceeded my expectations! My momma, you showed me the ways of prayer even when I didn't want to hear you praying. Thank you for your consistent support. My girls, Tyria, Malana, Terri, Seeds of Greatness women thank you for prayers and encouragement daily. Last but definitely not least, I thank God above all. Thanks for seeing me as Your Beloved when I saw nothing.

Introduction

The fact that you are even reading my words is a testimony. As a child, I was ALWAYS in church. From the age of about eight years old, I came to know God. However, I wasn't in relationship with Him until the age of thirty. For as long as I can remember, I was always shy, very timid, and quiet. I never wanted to do anything that would cause me to have to be in the spotlight. Still, I was confident in school, and reading was my escape. I had many friends, but I was never outgoing. I also grew up overweight, and I was uncomfortable in my own skin. Having this personality led me to doubt myself. Moreover, growing up and experiencing rejection caused me to be very needy with male relationships. My relationship with my natural father was one with minimal teaching on how a man is supposed to treat a woman. As a result, in my romantic relationships, I gave almost everyone a chance. I was searching for love, even if I saw some things that I didn't like, I overlooked them. My mindset was that they would love me because I loved them. On the contrary, in reality, I was just lost.

After losing weight and getting attention for my looks, I ended up pregnant. My first child was born in 2008, and I was alone! I didn't want to pursue a romantic relationship with his father because I jumped into a sexual relationship without even really knowing him. Again, my need for love was still tainted. Nevertheless, God blessed me with my son, and He kept us both alive through emergency surgery.

Even after seeing God's love for me at that moment, I still decided to test the waters again. Two years later, I had my daughter with another man. This was another quick pregnancy. After I had another life growing inside of me, I realized again that I was still searching for a natural love that wasn't satisfying me. My daughter was born in 2010, and the need was STILL there!

In 2012, after several meaningless relationships, I thought I had found the one. (*Sidebar:* Ladies, we **DO NOT** find the one. **HE FINDS US**!) My new mate and I got married within seventy days! Yes, I saw the red flags. Yes, I knew he wasn't going to be able to take care of me. However, I wanted marriage. I thought that if I couldn't satisfy the need for love through dating relationships, a lasting married would solve it! Again, I was wrong. Within in six months, the husband was kicked out of the house. I had taken myself and my two small children through tons of emotional torment because I was seeking the wrong god.

By 2014, I was sad, depressed, and I felt like a failure. What did I do at that moment? Did I choose to surrender to Christ?! Nope. Instead, I went back to school full-time to become a Registered Nurse. If you know anything about nursing school, you can imagine that it is stressful. After getting out of an emotionally bad marriage, I threw myself into school thinking that making more money to support my family would solve all of my problems. Yet again, I was wrong. That same year, after two years of trying, I was finally divorced. Feelings of condemnation were on me really heavily, but I didn't have time to deal with them. School was my main focus, and the light at the end of the tunnel was coming!

In January of 2015, my church (Seeds of Greatness Bible Church) started a program called Wives in Training. I received a mentor who I love dearly, and I was also able to fellowship with other Christian women. This was when things started to change. During that year, I still went back and forth with my ex-husband. I questioned if I should be divorced, should we get back together, was I wrong... I attempted to conduct my own marriage therapy through my lines of questioning. However, the one thing I was not doing was reading my Bible. How was I supposed to hear from God or even discern His voice if I wasn't reading His word? Thankfully, relief was on the way!

I finished school in May, graduated, and passed my state boards on the first try! At that point, I should have been ecstatic, but I was not. The smoke finally cleared from my busy-with-nothing life, and I realized that I was still depressed. I was depressed about having two children with two different men, depressed about being divorced, and now depressed that I couldn't find a better job. I was broken and I needed to find a way to pull myself out of that dark place and into a better life for myself and my children. Therefore, I began to listen to motivational speakers on social media in hopes that I would regain control of my heart. Finally, with all this brokenness came the Love that I was searching for ALL of my life!

I started following a young lady on Periscope, and I bought a Key Word Study Bible. I read it like it was a text book from school. Every night at work, I needed to be filled with what God was telling me. Since I had studied for nursing and wasn't satisfied, I told myself that I was going to study the word of God. I knew that His word would give me the insight that I needed to move forward and finally enjoy life. Moreover, I was able to fully experience the agape love of God. Even though we cannot physically see Him, He has loved us in ways that even our natural parents have not. He loves us despite the times when we ignored Him and put Him on a shelf. Still nothing you or I have done can separate us from His love.

My background story would not qualify me to write anything to anyone, but God qualifies us! After incorporating God's word into my life, this girl who used to be shy joined a self-publishing class in December of 2015 and fought to bring this devotional to you! Yes, YOU! The woman reading this may have been where I was. You may still be there, but I am here to let you know that you are coming out, BELOVED! This devotional was written for the woman who is tired of being frustrated. It's for the mother who cannot financially do it on her own or in her own strength. This book is for the woman who is so timid that she fears everything. It is also for the woman that has been divorced and feels guilty and ashamed. It's even for the woman who knows of God but does not have a relationship with Him. It is time that you change your mindset to the things of the Kingdom. There is no condemnation for those who are in Christ Jesus!

This 65-day devotional will take you on a new journey for you. With the help of Jesus Christ, you can move forward into your Kingdom Destiny and Purpose! You will renew your mind, and His word will transform your life. After transformation comes prosperity. God delights in the prosperity of His servants. Before you begin to read, I have a few suggestions to help you along the way:

1. If you have a friend that you can partner with, I suggest that you do that. (If not, it's okay.) The friend should be someone who needs a change and also who will be a cheerleader for you and vice versa.
2. Make sure you have a notebook so that you can write down what Holy Spirit reveals to you during this journey. It is also a good way to look back and see how you have improved. You can also pick up the His Beloved Journal!
3. DO NOT GIVE UP! There will be a community of encouraging women at www.genevajewel.com that can cheer you on when you think you should stop. We will also pray with you while you start your journey towards freedom. God sees you, Beloved, and He has been waiting for you; so surrender to Him.

Let's get started!

Praying continually,

Geneva

Salvation Prayer

Father God,

I come to you right now because I want to surrender. I surrender my will for yours. I believe that your son Jesus died on the cross for me and rose on the third day and is now alive with you and interceding for me every day. I place my life in your hands and I am ready to start this journey with you as my guide. I need your help and I ask for it today. I know that you dying on the cross saves me and I am a new creature in you. Old ways are put away and all things are becoming new right now.

In Jesus name, Amen

Holy Spirit

Jesus,

You said that you would send a comforter who would be my helper and my guide. I ask God that you fill me with Holy Spirit. I ask Holy Spirit that you speak to me clearly as I read the word and listen to You on a daily basis. Come commune with me. You are welcome in my heart and in my life. I thank You in advance for guidance and wisdom as I am on this journey of revelation. I am an open vessel and ready for you to pour into me.

In Jesus name, Amen

Contents

	Scripture References
Day 1	1 Corinthians 9:26-27 (MSG)
Day 2	Ephesians 1:3-4 (MSG)
Day 3	Ephesians 2:4 (MSG)
Day 4	Psalms 34:18 (MSG)
Day 5	Psalms 16:1 (KJV)
Day 6	2 Corinthians 5:17 (KJV)
Day 7	1 Corinthians 15:58 (AMP)
Day 8	Isaiah 26:3 (AMP)
Day 9	Proverbs 19:21 (MSG)
Day 10	Ephesians 6:12 (KJV)
Day 11	Romans 8:1 (KJV)
Day 12	Philippians 4:6 (KJV)
Day 13	2 Corinthians 10:5 (KJV)
Day 14	2 Corinthians 4:8-9 (KJV)
Day 15	James 1:8 (KJV)
Day 16	James 1:2-4 (KJV)
Day 17	James 1:19 (KJV)
Day 18	James 2:17 (KJV)
Day 19	Proverbs 11:14 (KJV)
Day 20	1 Peter 2:9 (KJV)
Day 21	Isaiah 61:7 (KJV)
Day 22	Luke 10:19 (KJV)
Day 23	Colossians 3:2 (KJV)
Day 24	John 16:33 (KJV)
Day 25	Job 22:28 (KJV)
Day 26	Luke 12:8 (KJV)
Day 27	Romans 8:28 (KJV)
Day 28	Romans 8:38-39 (KJV)

Day 29	Mark 12:30 (MSG)
Day 30	Psalms 51:10 (KJV)
Day 31	Proverbs 3:5-6 (KJV)
Day 32	2 Corinthians 12:9 (KJV)
Day 33	Jeremiah 29:11 (KJV)
Day 34	Luke 21:15 (AMP)
Day 35	Galatians 5:16 (KJV)
Day 36	1 Corinthians 10:13 (KJV)
Day 37	Psalms 37:4 (KJV)
Day 38	Matthew 6:33-34 (KJV)
Day 39	Hebrews 13:5 (KJV)
Day 40	1 Peter 2:9 (KJV)
Day 41	Deuteronomy 28:13 (KJV)
Day 42	Matthew 10:39 (MSG)
Day 43	Matthew 7:13-14 (KJV)
Day 44	Luke 6:47-49 (KJV)
Day 45	Matthew 11:28 (KJV)
Day 46	Romans 8:13 (KJV)
Day 47	Romans 8:31 (KJV)
Day 48	Matthew 17:20 (KJV)
Day 49	Malachi 3:10-11 (KJV)
Day 50	Psalms 55:22 (KJV)
Day 51	Matthew 19:26 (KJV)
Day 52	2 Corinthians 5:7 (KJV)
Day 53	2 Corinthians 3:17 (KJV)
Day 54	Proverbs 8:12 (AMP)
Day 55	Galatians 6:9 (KJV)
Day 56	Ephesians 3:20 (KJV)
Day 57	1 Peter 5:10 (AMP)
Day 58	Hebrews 11:6 (AMP)
Day 59	Deuteronomy 8:18 (AMP)

Day 60	Psalms 139:14 (AMP)
Day 61	Proverbs 8:35 (AMP)
Day 62	Joel 2:25 (KJV)
Day 63	Romans 12:2 (KJV)
Day 64	Proverbs 31:10 (AMP)
Day 65	3 John 1:2 (AMP)

Day 1

"I don't know about you, but I'm running hard for the finish line. I'm giving it everything I've got. No sloppy living for me! I'm staying alert and in top condition. I'm not going to get caught napping, telling everyone else all about it, and then missing out myself."
1 Corinthians 9:26-27 (MSG)

After I would go to the club with my girlfriends, I would always tell them that I was going to church in the morning. I also used to brag about paying my tithes. The one thing I didn't realize was that my verbal talk about being a Christian was not matching up to what I should have been doing or what God had assigned me to do. I wasn't giving God all that I had. I was actually playing God and using Him when I got into a bind. I was living sloppily, and it caught up to me. I tried many times to stop living for self. It took a while, but God stayed forgiving and accepted me every time with open arms. How many times have you started something and NEVER completed the original task? Have you returned to a dead relationship knowing that it was toxic for you and caused you to live sloppily? Maybe it was that New Year's resolution for weight loss that turned into weight gain... We all have done something that we regret, but the great thing about Jesus is that He forgives us. We even get the chance to start over!

Today is the beginning of a new journey for you. Set aside time each day during the next sixty-five days to sit in His presence. That time could be spent reading a book on Holy Spirit, reading one or two chapters a day in your Bible, or missing your favorite television show and giving that hour to God. Whatever you choose, stick with it for this allotted timeframe. Not only will God be pleased with you, but you will also become more equipped to walk in your true identity. You will learn that anything that you have purposed in your heart can be done. The most important ingredient for your success is your focus on God. You must run this race as if your life depends on it! (Actually, it does!)

Do not look back on yesterday, because today is a new day with new mercies. Make a decision to NOT live sloppily. Instead, stay on top of your game, and pursue your dreams and interests. In addition to telling people how good God is, how about you show them! Give God everything that you've got in order to complete the task, and He will reward your diligence. He is a rewarder of those who diligently seek Him.

Speak It:
- ♥ God equips me with EVERYTHING that I need to succeed!
- ♥ I will always be in top condition!
- ♥ I will complete every task that is set before me!

Day 2

"How blessed is God! And what a blessing He is! He's the Father of our Master, Jesus Christ, and takes us to high places of blessing in Him. Long before He laid down earth's foundations, He had US in mind, had settled on us as the focus of His love, to be made WHOLE and HOLY by His love."
Ephesians 1:3-4 (MSG)

    Love is a word that is used often and incorrectly. Has anyone ever told you that they loved you, but you felt broken and damaged in the end? The situation that you experienced was NOT love. Love is patient, kind, and it does not hurt. You must renew your mind to the correct meaning of what love really is. You were the center of God's interest or activity before He even started the earth! He loved you before you were even a thought. In fact, He loves you even when you do not love yourself. His love is so strong for you that it is designed to put you in an **<u>unbroken</u>** or **<u>undamaged</u>** state. It can even set you back in one piece as a cast does to mend a broken bone. His love will show you that you are valued. It will take time, but you will come out of this feeling refreshed.

    Meditating on the scripture above will help you start the foundation for mending your broken areas. During my journey of making faith a lifestyle and not just something that I did on Sundays, I've learned that I am different. The way that I think is different from the way the world thinks. With God's love towards me being in the front of my mind, I began to realize that I was not crazy for speaking faith when things seemed the opposite. Furthermore, I began to focus on His genuine love towards me despite all the things I had done. He knew every time that I would walk away from Him to do my own thing just to come right back in search of His love. Yet, He still loves me just as much as He loves you!

As you dedicate your life truly to Him, be grateful for His mercy and kindness. Take this time to separate yourself from things that were taking your focus off God. At times, it will seem like you are alone, but you are not. Another great thing about Jesus is that He sent us a comforter in Holy Spirit who is right by our side. As you go through this journey, you will become closer to Him. In addition, your relationship with God, Jesus, and Holy Spirit will change your life in tremendous ways! However, you must be willing to yield. Are you willing? Just in case you think you don't deserve His love, remember that NOTHING can separate you from the love of God. He knew you before you knew yourself, and He still sent His Son to die for you. Take a hold of your destiny today!

Speak It:
- ♥ My true identity is established in Christ!
- ♥ God loved me before the foundations of the earth!
- ♥ God has mended my broken heart and damaged areas!

"Instead, immense in mercy and with an incredible love, He embraced us. He took our sin-dead lives and made us alive in Christ."

Ephesians 2:4 (MSG)

    At this point, you may be saying to yourself, "Why am I doing this? I don't have time to dedicate to reading the Bible or even this devotional! I've done so much, been to the club way too many nights, had multiple abortions, and I've never finished anything before. So, why am I doing this now?" Let me tell you that He STILL loves you. The fact that you are reading this devotional and taking the time to renew your mind is what matters. What you also need to know is that He knew what you were going to do last week, and His incredible love has not changed towards you! When I was doing what I thought was okay - going to the club and then to church every Sunday - I was being double-minded. It led me into some relationships that were not good examples of love. At the time, I thought I was just having fun. However, what I was really doing was conforming to the world and not in Christ. I wanted a man of God, but I went to places where I wouldn't be blessed with what God had for me. Through my experiences, I've learned that God does not bless my mess. He did keep me safe, but I was naïve to think that I was going to find a life partner in that atmosphere. I didn't know the true meaning of love, nor did I know my true identity at that point.

    While writing this devotional, I was attacked on many levels. The main attack was in my thinking. The enemy of our soul knows that we will be able to defeat him once we tap into our true potential and get a glimpse of how powerful we are in Christ. The enemy likes to keep our minds cluttered with self-doubt. I had to overcome those thoughts to get these words to you! Christ took my sin-dead life and made me alive in Him. It took a long time for me to see this, and I need you to see that you don't have to be naïve. He doesn't hold your past against you. On the contrary, He embraces you each day with new mercies. You must see that for yourself and let Him reawaken you. Whatever you have done that has caused you to think that you are less than eligible for His love, let it go NOW! Remember, He knew you before you were even born, and He loves you anyway!

Speak It:
- ♥ I will not let my past hinder me from moving into my future!
- ♥ I am made alive in Christ!
- ♥ I accept God's love towards me!

Day 4

"If your heart is broken, you'll find God right there; if you're kicked in the gut, he'll help you catch your breath."

Psalms 34:18 (MSG)

What is the current status of your heart? Is it broken, or has someone or something hit you so hard that you can't seem to catch your breath? The wind was knocked out of me when I found out that my ex-husband was in a relationship with another woman. I even had pictures to prove it. I remember crying so hard on my cold kitchen floor. It seemed that I couldn't catch my breath. I felt alone and unwanted. Although I didn't feel it at the moment, God was right there. It took me almost two years to realize that. I was so caught up in what I saw on television and in the movies that I never took time to go to the source. The source I'm referring to is the Bible.

    I regret living twelve years of my adult life without reading it. As a result of not reading my Bible, it took so long for me to see my true identity in Christ. If I did read my Bible, it was only on Sunday while the pastor was preaching. Because of this, I was not equipped with the knowledge of what my Heavenly Father had already done for me. However, God always gets His will in the end. When I think of the saying "Knowledge is Power," I realize that it's definitely true. You have the power already within you to defeat the enemy. You have the power within you to accomplish your dreams, to start your own business, or just get over a broken heart.

I know it may not seem like it at the moment, but He is there with you right now! Whatever your situation may be, you can find God there waiting for you to call on Him. Cry out to Him, and He will heal your broken heart. You will be able to stand up and triumph when it's all over. Please do not wait to open your Bible. Yes, you will be different from your friends, co-workers, and maybe even your family for focusing on the word of God. Still, it can change your life and theirs as well. Do not let your schedule influence your relationship with God. You can start small with a chapter a day and fifteen minutes of prayer. Just be consistent, and He will meet you where you need Him the most! Remember, He is right there with you. Seek Him.

Speak It:
- ♥ God is with me, and I am healed!
- ♥ God is my restorer!
- ♥ I seek God daily!

Day 5

"Preserve me, O God, for in thee do I put my trust."
Psalms 16:1 (KJV)

The word *preserve* in the Greek-Hebrew translation means "to watch, to keep, to guard, to be careful, to watch carefully over, and to be on one's guard." (*Key Word Study Bible*, AMG Publishers) I've learned through my journey with Jesus that I must speak out of my mouth what I want. On this fifth day of your journey, I pray that you have been verbalizing the confessions up to date. The fact that you are even reading this is proof that what you speak comes to life. I needed and still need God to preserve me. I needed Him to keep my mind when the images of my ex-husband's infidelity kept coming back to me repeatedly. I needed Him to condition my mind to be comfortable with developing Geneva. I also needed to realize that I was more than just a mother. Furthermore, I needed to focus on my relationship with Christ before I could focus on one with the man of God that He has just for me. I needed God to keep me focused on what my purpose was in Him so that I could write this for you.

Keep in mind that there has to be trust in order to have any relationship. When you pray to God and see yourself changing, when you wake up happy to get the day started, when you finally do things that you have dreamed and maybe even things that you could never think of, they are all results of those prayers and your trust in God. Still, you must have a relationship with Him. You know that if you were in a physical relationship with someone and it was one sided, it would be hard to trust that person. Moreover, I don't think the relationship would last long. Thank God for not being like man! He doesn't keep record of the times when our relationship with Him was null and void. So start that personal and intimate relationship with Him now, if you have not already done so, and stay committed. When you know that He will never lead you into any harm, you will live a life of freedom. Give all your cares to Him!

Speak It:
- ♥ I trust God!
- ♥ I am preserved by God!
- ♥ I cast all my cares on God!

Day 6

"Therefore, if any man be in Christ, he is a new creature, old things are passed away; behold, all things are become new."

2 Corinthians 5:17 (KJV)

Once you focus on getting your life and ways dedicated to God, it seems like everything either goes haywire, or you think that you have made the wrong decision. DO NOT LET THAT STOP YOU! As the scripture says, you are a new creature, everything about the old you has passed away, and everything is new. You must believe that the word of God is law. Whatever it says about you is the truth, and you must walk in it. It does take time to wrap your natural mind around this, and that is okay. However, just do not dwell on the past. Don't even think about what you didn't do yesterday. Each day, we receive new mercies and new grace from God. I don't know about you, but I am excited about that!

I can remember always being upset about raising my two children without a man in the home. I was frustrated about picking them up from school alone, dealing with bloody noses alone, going to events alone, and I was getting frustrated with them. I would cry out to God, "Please forgive me for choosing this for them. Forgive me for yelling at them when it's not their fault that the relationships were not meant to be."

I prayed that many times until I realized that I am new in Christ. Once I really believed that, I walked in it every day. Even if yesterday wasn't a good day, I never spoke against what this scripture says. The peace and patience that I needed was already in me. I just had to wrap my natural mind around that fact. The most important thing you should know is that you control yourself. We decide to sleep late and not pray or to overeat and not work out. The old ways of thinking cannot live in your new life. Whatever is keeping you from walking in your newness in Christ, let it go today and don't look back. Remember, you are in Christ and all things are new!

Speak It:
- ♥ I am a new creature in Christ!
- ♥ I speak only what the word of God says that I am!
- ♥ I am blessed!

Day 7

"Therefore, my beloved brethren, be firm (steadfast), immovable, always abounding in the work of the Lord [always being superior, excelling, doing more than enough in the service of the Lord], knowing and being continually aware that your labor in the Lord is not futile [it is never wasted or to no purpose]."

1 Corinthians 15:58 (AMP)

It has been a week since you started on this journey. Is it going as planned? Have you been tempted to quit? Maybe it's been going well, and you have no complaints. I'd be shocked by the latter. I say that because it seemed like when I got determined enough for God, anything that could present itself would. I just wasn't aware that it was an attack from the devil. If something or someone from your past comes at you during this time, I'd suggest that you tell them it's not a good time. The devil only knows the old. He won't send anything new; he will only tempt you with what you "think" you like.

My temptation was being in a relationship. For as long as I can remember, I was always wanting a relationship. That caused me to accept things and people that I would not have accepted had I been steadfast in my beliefs and submission to Christ. From 2009 until 2015, I attempted about four times to dedicate six months to God, and I never did it. During those six years, I had another child out of wedlock, a couple more failed relationships, and then a marriage that was the worst pain I think I have ever felt. I was being led by sight rather than by faith. Never let what you see affect you. I know it may be hard to do, but that is what kept me stuck and bound for six years! It is not crazy for you to excel in the things of Christ. It's not crazy that you don't go out and get drunk. It's perfectly fine that you like to go to Bible Study and Sunday service and that you fast to overcome your flesh. You are different in Christ and that is perfectly okay. Stay committed and immovable!

I wouldn't trade my pain because it pushed me into my purpose. In fact, I would have made it here anyway if I was pursuing Christ as I am now. Let me explain one thing about today's scripture. It's not telling you to become a preacher, unless God is leading you. What it's saying is that whatever you do for Him, and do it with excellence. If you have a blog, set a schedule and keep it updated. If you are in the choir, sing as if you are on tour. Give God your all! In reality, we can never give Him enough praise for what He has done for us and what He continues to do. Remember, your labor is NOT in vain. It may seem hard, and it's not the popular thing to do, but God will grace you. He will show off in your life if you show up for Him.

Speak It:
- ♥ I am steadfast and immovable, always abounding in the Lord!
- ♥ My identity is defined in Christ!
- ♥ What I do for Christ is never wasted or without purpose.

Day 8

> *"You will guard him and keep him in perfect and constant peace whose mind [both its inclination and its character] is stayed on You, because he commits himself to You, leans on You, and hopes confidently in You."*
>
> Isaiah 26:3 (AMP)

Today should be the beginning of a great week for you! I pray that you are really spending as much quality time with God as you can. The work that He can do in us is amazing! Now, I would like to know the condition of your mind. Do you have sleepless nights? Are you worried about bills, your children, your spouse, how you look, or if you will ever get married? There are many things that can take our minds off God, but we must keep our focus on Him. Think about Him, meditate on His word and confess it. When you do this, it becomes real in your life. You will begin to have so much confidence in God that NOTHING can stop you! When you commit to Him, He will be that shoulder that you need to lean on when you feel low. He will be the hope you need to make it through the day. He will also be the peace that you need to rock you to sleep at night.

You also need to evaluate your character. I believed in God, but my character showed something different. I would say a little travel prayer maybe every other day, but I didn't really believe that I could have what God said was mine. In reality, I was a dead Christian. I wasn't vibrant; I was broken, and I was doing everything that the people in the world were doing. Therefore, it never worked out for me. I wanted to really feel God's love for me, but my character was out of line. When I made the decision to change what I was doing, I began to hear from God in a mighty way. No, it was not easy to stop what I thought was fun. It was difficult to stop going out with friends that I had been with every weekend. However, I was tired of being depressed, and I was tired of being a dead Christian.

It's time that you live in constant peace. Now is the time that you lean on God, rather than yourself or others. Confident hope in God equals Faith. Without faith, it is impossible to please God. Make a choice today to keep your mind on God, and let Him change your character from the inside out. Remember, He WILL give you peace that surpasses your understanding.

Speak It:
- In peace, I lay down and sleep at night!
- I am not worried about anything, because my trust is in God!
- God provides me with peace that surpasses all my understanding!

"We humans keep brainstorming options and plans, but God's purpose prevails."

Proverbs 19:21 (MSG)

Do you sit around and try to figure everything out? Maybe you think to yourself, "If I get this job, life will be better. If I lose ten more pounds, that will make me feel better. Maybe once I have a good man to help with the kids, everything will balance out." The problem is all in the way you're making plans for your life. Stop planning without seeking God first. I had a ton of ideas and solutions in mind for myself, but they never worked. NEVER! Like I mentioned before, I would have relationships for a little less than a year, and then we would break up. However, the people who I hung out with would be in long-lasting relationships for years! During that time, I was looking with my "natural" eye. As a result, I was jealous that they had someone and I didn't.

If you are like me, you've probably gotten tired of being sad all the time. All you genuinely want is to wake up and be content - even if you are not where you want to be at the moment. I had to realize that I wanted to please God above all things. Yes, my friends had significant others just as I desired. However, I knew that I didn't want to commit fornication or live with another man before I was married. I had done all of that before. In addition, I didn't just want anybody. I knew God had a mate just for me. I just had to be patient and wait for Him to send my mate. During this time, I even took a job that was not ideal just because I thought the money would make me feel better. Nevertheless, I hated it, I had to go to work miserable for months until I was blessed with another job.

You see, I was doing all the planning, and Geneva's plan had a 100% failure rate. I wasn't being led by God. In Jeremiah 29:11, we see that God knows the thoughts that He has for us and our expected end. We often try to plan everything out on our own. I did that for eleven years, and it caused me a lot of heartache and pain. Yet, God's purpose for my life still prevailed. I encourage you to stop brainstorming and seek God for your purpose. Don't live another moment without His guidance in every area of your life. When He is leading, you will be at perfect peace. Remember, He knows your expected end, and it does not include anything that would cause you pain.

Speak It:
- ♥ I hear from God clearly!
- ♥ God is the planner of my life!
- ♥ I live out my purpose in God!

Day 10

> "For we wrestle not against flesh and blood, but against principalities, against powers, against the rulers of darkness of the world, against spiritual wickedness in high places."
>
> Ephesians 6:12 (KJV)

Don't let this scripture scare you, but I need to let you in on a couple of things. When I decided to keep my focus on God and not date, it was hard. For the most part, I knew that I didn't want to be married to another man like the one I had before. Instead, I wanted a man who loved God more than he loved me. I also wanted him to acknowledge God in all his ways. My standards about marriage changed once I realized that it was more about purpose and destiny than love. However, being lonely was something that bothered me. So, I will be honest and let you know that I went back and forth with my ex-husband for two years after we broke up. Besides not wanting to be alone, I did that for seven-hundred and thirty-five days because I thought that he would change. For some reason, I thought that his change would be a result of knowing how much I really wanted the marriage to work. When I finally decided to let go, he kept coming back and wanting to try again. He would even come to my church with other women, and I would be sitting in the row right behind them. How ironic is that?

It was actually strategic. If you didn't know, the devil is the ruler of evil things in this world. I also mentioned before that he only brings old things to you; he can never come with something new. He knew that it would bother the old me to see my ex-husband with another woman. It actually made me angry to the point that I got down on my knees and prayed. I prayed for my deliverance, girl! I knew that I didn't want to be with him, but the fact that he was in *my* house (my church lol), dressed nice with another woman made me mad. This came after he asked for counseling and I turned him down because I was getting myself together. In actuality, I knew it was another lie. He didn't love me; he was being used by the devil. I realized at that moment that I wasn't fighting against him. I was fighting against the spirits that were using him and living inside of him. However, I was determined to win, because greater is He that is in me than he that is in this world!

Do you wonder why people are mean to you and fight you all the time - especially when you are living for God? Girl, you've been praying these last couple of days, actively reading your word, and changing the way you think. Then, here comes somebody or some situation trying to test you! Well, I'm here to let you know that you will pass this test! Don't fight with your hands. Open up your mouth and pray! Call those things that are not as though they already are. Cast grudges, bitterness, and resentment out of your heart and mind! After I saw my ex-husband at my church that day, I prayed to be Spirit-led. I was walking in my own emotions, and that was not how I wanted to continue. It became my goal to see him and just smile, knowing that I had overcome another thing that the devil tried to use to destroy me. No matter what keeps coming at you, keep fighting. Remember,

God always causes us to have the victory, but we must use the right tools!!

Speak It:
- ♥ I acknowledge God in all my ways!
- ♥ I am not of this world!
- ♥ I am victorious!

Day 11

"There is therefore now no condemnation to them which are in Christ Jesus, who walk not after the flesh but after the Spirit."

Romans 8:1 (KJV)

Condemnation can be defined as "a sentencing or a strong disapproval." (www.dictionary.com) The Greek-Hebrew definition is "the process of judging." (*The Key Word Study Bible*, AMG Publishers) How often do you judge yourself? If you are like the old me, you probably condemn yourself for everything. If my children got sick, I thought I was a bad parent. My daughter was slightly overweight, and I thought I was killing her slowly. If I didn't eat right, I felt like I was never going to lose weight. My marriage didn't work, so I felt like I didn't try hard enough. There are many things that you can say to yourself that are contrary to who you are in Christ.

One day, I realized that I had to literally walk after the Spirit. I couldn't slack on making home cooked meals for my children. So what I was raising them full-time by myself. I couldn't use that as an excuse anymore. When I ate something that I shouldn't have eaten, I had to look at the emotions behind it. Was I sad? Was I sleepy? What was causing me to crave some food for comfort? I had to consistently ask God to help me manage my time so I could cook more. I needed Him to help me keep my mouth away from unnecessary foods when I was emotional. Additionally, I had to cast down those thoughts that I was a failure in that marriage.

Whatever you are saying to yourself that is condemning you, make a decision to stop right now! You are a new creature in Christ, and there is no judgement against you. If you make a mistake, acknowledge it and get back up. Don't wallow in it and have a pity party. Look at the emotions that were involved in the circumstances, and be determined to react differently if it happens again. When you seek God and Holy Spirit who is our helper and our guide, He will provide you with all the knowledge and comfort that you need. It is essential that you stay connected with God and read your Bible daily. In order to walk after the Spirit, you must recognize what Jesus and His Father God are like. Once you have an idea of their qualities, you will be able to discern Holy Spirit from your flesh. Remember, seek after the Spirit and do not attempt to satisfy your flesh! We are in this race to win, and our reward is eternal life!

Speak It:
- ♥ I walk after the Spirit and not the Flesh!
- ♥ There is now no condemnation, because I am in Christ Jesus!
- ♥ I include God in every area of my life!

Day 12

"Be careful for nothing, but in everything by prayer and supplication with thanksgiving, let your request be made known unto God."

Philippians 4:6 (KJV)

How is your prayer life at this point? I know that you are praying daily, but what are you praying about? How are you praying? I need you to give everything to God in prayer. Supplication in the Greek-Hebrew is defined as "a petition." (The Key Word Study Bible, AMG Publishers) A petition can be defined as "making a formal request to someone in authority." (www.dictionary.com) Praise the Lord that you have direct access to the Most High God! My prayer life changed when I started really getting into the Word. I read it in books, I read at work, and I stopped watching television to make more time for reading His Word. My life was settled around getting as much in me so that I could be prepared to fight! When I was able to say without stammering that I am the head and not the tail, that I am blessed coming in and going out, that His favor surrounds me like a shield, that He gives me power to trample on scorpions and serpents, and nothing shall by any means harm me, I felt empowered when I prayed.

It was exciting for me to have a conversation with God. I knew that He was listening, because He hears the heartfelt fervent prayer of the righteous. When I pray His word and await a response, He is not like man; He cannot lie. Those things that I declared and decreed were established unto me. I read the Word and meditated on it. Accordingly, it flowed out of me, and that's what I stood on as my foundation. Now, some of my prayers weren't answered right away. However, when they were, it was like waves of blessings kept knocking me down! I also prayed with thanksgiving. It is not uncommon to cry out to God in desperation. I've had many of those moments. However, I've prayed more prayers of thanksgiving after that.

Do not go to God sulkily. Go boldly and make your formal request to Him with thanksgiving in your heart. Even if your situation isn't ideal, when you go to Him with thanksgiving, you are using your Faith muscles. We know that Faith pleases God. In everything that you think about doing, take it to God. If you want a new job, take it to Him. Thank Him for the new job even though it hasn't manifested yet. You will notice that He may even lead you to the right website for your desired job. The right person might come across your path, or you will have favor that no one else was given just to put you in that position. It may seem like a lot to pray to God about everything. Contrarily, what has not praying got you? Take time to be still and listen to His voice. Remember, He hears your prayers, and His eyes are over you. Let Him bless you with an abundance when you take everything to Him first.

Speak It:
- ♥ God hears my heartfelt fervent prayers!
- ♥ God's word does not return void!
- ♥ I meditate on the word day and night!

Day 13

> *"Casting down imaginations, and every high thing that exalteth itself against the knowledge of God, and bringing into captivity every thought to the obedience of Christ."*
>
> 2 Corinthians 10:5 (KJV)

Have you ever made the statement that your mind is racing? Do your thoughts keep you up at night? Do old memories creep in from time to time and make you second guess yourself? I have said in my past plenty of times that I had so much on my mind that I couldn't get to sleep the night before. I would see old memories when I closed my eyes. They would be memories of old relationships, the Instagram pictures of my ex-husband and the woman who was "just his friend," or thoughts of how I wouldn't be able to take care of my children financially. All these imaginations would cause fear, worry, doubt, and unbelief to overwhelm me. I can remember thinking about the times when I used to be so happy and I could fall asleep so easily. I even wondered what was wrong with me.

The thing is, I wasn't casting down those thoughts and imaginations that were totally against the will of God. This was because I didn't read the Bible, and I didn't know that I had the authority to speak the word to my situations. I will remind you again that Jeremiah 29:11 says that God's thoughts towards me are thoughts of peace and not of evil, to give me an expected end. When I realized that God thinks peace towards me and that He wants to give me the future I hoped for, I asked myself why my thinking was the opposite! At that moment, I decided that when any oppressing thought or situation would come to me, I would call it by name, and then quote Jeremiah 29:11.

I made this a consistent part of my plan to rebuke the plans of Satan from my life. I still do it to this day! The devil will bring the thoughts, the images, and the memories back to you. You just need to understand that you have the authority to bring them into the obedience of Jesus Christ. This is why it is so very important to refrain from conforming to this world. We must not get too busy and forget to spend time with God. It is essential to the wellbeing of your life that you read His word. Let it take root in you so that you will have your sword ready when the devil comes to fight you! In fact, you will be renewed in Christ! Your mind won't be so bombarded with doubt and worry because you know who you are in Christ. Make a commitment today to cast down anything that comes to you that is not in the will of God. Your life should be one overflowing with joy, because you know that the joy of the Lord is your strength! Remember, God's thoughts towards you are of peace not of evil.

Speak It:
- ♥ God knows my expected end!
- ♥ The joy of the Lord is my strength!
- ♥ I bring into captivity every thought to the obedience of Christ!

Day 14

"We are troubled on every side, yet not distressed; we are perplexed, but not in despair; persecuted, but not forsaken; cast down but not destroyed."
2 Corinthians 4:8-9 (KJV)

A great deal of my pain has been emotional. My heart always seemed to be broken or in the process of being broken. What type of pain have you been dealing with? Has it seemed like every time you try to get ahead, there is some type of trouble everywhere you turn? Is your mind puzzled or confused? These things can be happening to you, but they do not have the power to affect your mood when you know that God has your back. You may work at a job where you have trouble daily. You could be dealing with a boss that is rude and mean to you. That person may cause you to suffer from anxiety when it's time to go to work. The devil may bring thoughts of confusion to you, which is not of God, but you are not hopeless. You know that God has a plan for you. Do not get caught in the trap and begin to wonder if what you are doing for God is worth it.

You are in your word daily, speaking affirmations, and praying the word of God. You even dropped your old friends and your old ways. Then, someone who isn't following God's will gets engaged, gets the promotion you wanted, gets a new car when you're riding the bus, or does anything that would make you doubt why you are living different from everybody else. Don't let what someone else is doing cause you to lose that hope! Keep moving forward in Christ, and be steadfast. Treat this relationship like the relationship with homeboy who broke your heart. How many chances did you give him? How many times did you go back to him when he was doing you wrong? God has NEVER lied to you, He has never broken your heart, nor has He ever deserted you. Don't you think He deserves for you to keep chasing Him?!

Maybe someone is persistently making it their business to annoy you. Is the father of your child or children making it hard to communicate? Maybe he doesn't want to help you financially, let alone spend time with your child or children. This trouble can be very annoying, but God has not abandoned you. He is Jehovah Jireh, the God that is your provider! He will provide for you on all levels. Could your pain be from someone walking out on you? Did your mom or dad leave you? Did your husband walk out and never look back? Maybe someone has rejected you for having an abortion. The scripture lets you know that even after those events in your life, you are not rendered useless! You are NOT destroyed! Your Heavenly Father loves you more than you can wrap your mind around. He has given you Holy Spirit as your helper and your guide. We must tap into Him! There will be tests in life, especially as a Christian. Still, we are equipped to fight and win! The situation that you are overcoming is making your faith in Christ stronger! Remember, you are above only and not beneath!

Speak It:
- ♥ I walk by Faith and not by sight!
- ♥ The Lord causes me to triumph!
- ♥ In my weakness, I am made strong through Christ!
- ♥ I am steadfast and immovable!

Day 15

"A double-minded man is unstable in all his ways."
James 1:8 (KJV)

The Greek-Hebrew translation for double-minded is "two-spirited, inconsistent, and wavering." (The Key Word Study Bible, AMG Publishers) Have you ever made a decision and couldn't stick with it? Have you set a goal for yourself and continuously went back and forth about it? I was double-minded about plenty of things. I realize now that I had no real faith in God during those times. I said many times that I wasn't going back to the club after I had a bad night, but I went back anyway. I went back and forth with my ex-husband for almost two years! I knew every time what the outcome would be. Yet, I would feel like trash on the way home, or I would feel foolish that next evening when he didn't answer my calls. I would go back to him, because I didn't have faith that God would send me a man of God. I was blinded by thinking that he would change, but I was the one who needed to change. I was constantly wavering, and it made my life miserable. I needed to see myself in a different light, and I needed to know how precious I was to God. Unfortunately, I didn't read the Bible at that time. Therefore, I wasn't equipped to fight. I was always confused on what I should do. One thing I knew for sure was that confusion is not from God; for the Bible tells us that "Where the spirit of the Lord is there is liberty." (2 Corinthians 3:17)

When you are double-minded, you never really have any freedom. My emotions were a wreck, and I didn't know how to stop. What area in your life is consumed by the spirit of doublemindedness? Have you had enough of feeling miserable? I got to the point where I was so broken that the only thing I could do was give myself to God. I made a decision to stop going to the clubs. I knew that I didn't want anyone from there, and I started to feel more and more uncomfortable. I also made the decision to stay away from my ex-husband, especially sexually. I started reading the Bible more than I had ever read it in my whole life. I dedicated my spare time to studying His word like I studied when I was in school to be a Registered Nurse.

I had to get my mind, soul, and emotions back on track. I was successful with God's help. I know that You can do it, too! It's not God's will for you not to accomplish your dreams because you get discouraged. It's also not His will for you to be in any relationship that causes you pain or challenges you to violate your relationship with Him. Decide today to be steadfast in everything that you do. Get into His word, and let it consume you. In addition, start using that faith muscle; it is a definite way to please God and crucify your flesh. Remember, without faith, it's impossible to please God.

Speak It:
- ♥ My faith brings forth patience!
- ♥ I trust God to lead me!
- ♥ I am steadfast!
- ♥ I am stable-minded!

Day 16

> *"My brethren, count it all joy when ye fall into divers temptations. Knowing this, that the trying of your faith worketh patience. But let patience have her perfect work, that ye may be perfect and entire, wanting nothing."*
>
> James 1:2-4 (KJV)

I'm sure that you have heard the saying, "Patience is a virtue." Well, it was a virtue that I did not have. I always wanted what I wanted right then and there. However, I found out that having a relationship with God doesn't really work like that. I would get frustrated when I felt like I was being tested. If I didn't get a job that I wanted, I would wonder why I had to stay at that job, instead of thinking that maybe God had a better job lined up for me. I would ask myself why a particular person would keep coming into my life. Instead, I should have refrained from entertaining the situation. I should have realized that saying no to temptation is only making me stronger. Instead of getting upset when the child support stopped, I should have been trusting God to provide all that I needed because I was a tither and an offering giver.

When we are in situations, we tend to want to have a pity party. What we don't realize is that everything that we go through when we are doing what we should as a Christian is only making us strong and preparing us for what God has for us. He wants us to use our faith and have a great deal of patience as well. If you are impatient, you are not walking by faith. When we use faith, it increases our patience. When patience is working on us, we will become whole, lacking and wanting nothing! If you are looking for a job, and it hasn't come yet, continue to thank God with a pure heart for the job that you have. If you don't have a job, thank Him for the one that is coming! If you are waiting for a husband, continue to have patience so that you can be whole when the man that God has for you finds you. Do not make the mistake that I made of going into a marriage broken!

As I write this to you, I am going through a test of patience myself. However, I am choosing to keep going so that I can pass this test. Whatever your test or temptation is, continue to trust God. Let patience work in your life, knowing that you will be whole and equipped to stand strong when the next temptation tries to come at you again! Remember, wholeness is at the end of this test!

Speak It:
- ♥ I am patient!
- ♥ I am complete and whole in God!
- ♥ I will pass this test!

Day 17

"Wherefore, my beloved brethren, let every man be swift to hear, slow to speak, slow to wrath."
James 1:19 (KJV)

The Greek-Hebrew word for wrath is orge, which means "anger, indignation, or vengeance." (The Key Word Study Bible, AMG Publishers) How quickly do you reply when you are speaking to someone? When you are in a heated conversation is your goal to win and be heard or to understand where the other person is coming from? I wasn't a good listener when it came to conversations. I was always on the defense, especially in personal relationships. I always wanted to be right, and I didn't want to get my feelings hurt. Basically, I was very selfish, and it didn't help. I even had to check myself when it came to the relationships with my children's fathers. There was turmoil, hurt, pain, and anger for years. One day, I literally gave what was provoking all those emotions to God. The provoking substance was fear. I was afraid that I wasn't going to be able to financially support them on my own, even though I was a tither and an offering giver! How silly is that! I was afraid that I would always have to take care of them alone, and they wouldn't have a father figure in the home. Fear led me to be hardheaded, to over talk people, and to get angry really quickly. This didn't happen just with their fathers. It also would happen at work and with girlfriends.

How are your personal relationships? Do you lose friends easily? Do you ever apologize first? Being a

Christian doesn't mean that you are only nice in church. It means that in everything you do, you show the characteristics of Christ. Take a moment when you are in an argument, and listen to the other person. Think about your response before you begin to speak. The Bible tells us that vengeance is the Lord's. (Deuteronomy 32:35) I've learned to let Him handle everything for me. Stop wasting your time harboring anger for people who are not even thinking about you! Remember, out of the heart the mouth speaks. So listen carefully to what you say. If you are speaking words of anger, check yourself and change it!

Speak It:
- ♥ I am slow to speak, slow to wrath, and swift to hear!
- ♥ The Lord fights all my battles!
- ♥ I walk in love daily!
- ♥ I fear NOTHING!

Day 18

> *"Even so faith, if it hath not works, is dead, being alone."*
>
> James 2:17 (KJV)

I never really had true faith in God. I was faithfully going to church and listening to the word, but if I didn't get what I wanted, Geneva made it happen. I did not trust God for increase even though I was a tither. I didn't even speak life over my money or any situation. I was consistently saying, "I'm broke." That is a definite NO! Faith means that you trust God. I trusted my mom 100%. I knew that she had my back, she loved me, and she would come if I needed her. However, I didn't trust God 100%, although He loved me BEFORE I was even in my mother's womb! The love that God demonstrates in His word is greater than human love. So why don't you trust Him with every fiber of your being? My reason was because I wanted everything instantly, and that is NOT how God works. It says in Hebrews 11:6 that it is impossible to please God without faith.

I don't know about you, but I want to be pleasing to my Father. If I don't trust Him, He's not pleased with me. He's not pleased with you either if you have more faith in yourself than you have in Him. You must step out on faith and show Him that you realize that you can't live life without Him. You can't make supernatural miracles and favor come from man like He can! Stop thinking so much about the money, and pay your tithes first, if you are not currently doing so. That is a faith step right there.

I know it may be tight financially right now, but giving God His ten percent will show Him that you have faith that He will make it work for your good. Stop worrying about your next move and talk to God. Listen for His answer and stop using your human logic when you have supernatural blood flowing through your veins! Oh, I hope you didn't forget that you are the King's kid! You are entitled to a supernatural extension of benefits, Queen. Step out on faith, and get ready to receive everything God has for you! Remember, put in faith work for your Father, and you will never be "laid-off."

Speak It:
- ♥ I have unshakeable faith!
- ♥ I walk by faith!
- ♥ I have a supernatural extension of benefits!

Day 19

*"Where no counsel is, the people fall:
but in the multitude of counsellors there is safety."*
                             Proverbs 11:14 (KJV)

When I think of a counselor, I picture someone helping me make good decisions. I have learned through this process of getting closer to God that I should have wise counsel. Not every person that gives you counsel is wise. We, as queens in Christ, need to surround ourselves with people who give safe counsel. This may not always be the current friends that you have. I have a great mentor at my church who is very down to earth. She has a solid relationship with God, so it was easy for me to accept her safe counsel. I had to learn that some of the people that I called friend did not give me sound biblical counsel. In order to transform and restore your thinking, you have to surround yourself with people who know the word of God. You must also know it for yourself. There's nothing against those friends, but for my sake and where I needed to be in my purpose and destiny in Christ, I had to learn to stop asking them for advice about anything.

Who is counseling you? Do you have any counsel at all? This scripture lets us know that we will fall without counsel. If you are someone who does not receive counsel, what is the reason behind that? Do you not trust people? Are you set in your ways and being stubborn? I did not have any premarital counseling before I got married to my ex-husband, and I am 100%

sure that I would not have gotten married if I had received counseling. The lack of counseling led to a fall in my life. Thank God for grace, mercy and a second chance!

Make a decision today to see if you can find a mentor at your church. When I felt like I had no friends, I prayed for kingdom relationships. As a result, God has blessed me with a good circle of friends. If you are shy, take a step out on faith and be bold. Ask God to connect you with the right people, and He will do it. Remember, the word says that "my people are destroyed because they lack knowledge." (Hosea 4:6) If you don't have any counsel, it may be easy for you to fall for the devil's trap every time. Be ready to change your mindset with the safe counselling that you will receive from your mentor.

Speak It:
- ♥ I have kingdom relationships!
- ♥ I only listen to wise counsel!
- ♥ I overflow with wisdom!

Day 20

"But ye are a chosen generation, a royal priesthood, a holy nation, a peculiar people, that ye should shew forth the praises of him who hath called you out of darkness into his marvelous light."

1 Peter 2:9 (KJV)

I have been calling you a Queen for a reason. Yes, I know in the human sense you may not be a queen. However, you were born again because Christ died for your sins. Since He is the King of Kings and you are His daughter, I think that makes you a Queen for sure! In fact, it's about time that you start acting like it! Don't worry, I also had to transform myself into behaving like a queen. You see, I always felt out of place. I've mentioned before that my relationships were different from my friends' relationships. They just didn't work out for me. I always knew that I wanted more, but I didn't know that I deserved it. I was ashamed when I had my second child out of wedlock, and that stopped me from going to church. I loved God, but I didn't know my true identity since I was not in His word.

Do you feel out of place? Do you feel like you are different from other people? I'll remind you again that it's true! You don't fit in the world because you are not of it. You are chosen by God, you are royalty, you are sacred, and you belong exclusively to Him. You just need to walk in it! When you realize that it's okay to want to be celibate until you're married, and that it's okay to live by what the Bible says and not be a selective Christian (one who believes certain things but not all things in the Bible), you will begin to walk with your head held higher. Nothing and no one will be able to make you feel inferior, because you will know who you are. People will ask why you are suddenly so happy and full of life. At that point, you will explain to them that your true identity has been revealed to you. You will no longer be in darkness, you will no longer let condemnation and fear rule over you. God is calling you out of the darkness, Queen! Remember, He chose you before the foundations of the earth, and He has been waiting for you to come back.

Speak It:
- ♥ I am a chosen generation!
- ♥ I am royalty!
- ♥ I am an heir according to the promise!

Day 21

"For your shame ye shall have double; and for confusion they shall rejoice in their portion: therefore, in their land they shall possess the double: everlasting joy shall be unto them."
Isaiah 61:7 (KJV)

I've had some great accomplishments in my life, but I've also had many days where I was ashamed. I was a habitual quitter. I started college over five times and quit. Sometimes, I used the excuse that it was too cold, so I didn't go to class. I was attending some classes but not all. I would quit a job whenever I wanted to, especially before I had children. I ran from anything that took me out of my comfort zone. This caused me to never complete anything I started. After getting pregnant with my second child, I went back to school and completed a certification program and became a Licensed Practical Nurse. I also went on to finish RN school. Once I completed one task, I knew that I could do anything I put my mind to. When I became frustrated with my life, I would read the beginning scripture. It literally gave me a ton of hope. I was ashamed of my mistakes, failures, and I tired of being confused.

It was amazing to know that He would still bless me, even though I stepped out of His will. The best part for me was knowing that I would have everlasting joy! Going from depressed to everlasting joy is amazing. Even as I write this to you, I am filled with joy because it is giving me peace, and it's a part of my purpose. If I had not gotten into the word of God, I would still be lost. I encourage you, Queen, to pick your head up and know that God has a redemption plan for your life! You must trust Him enough to give Him your time. Whatever was taken from you will be given back with a double portion! Focus on His word, and let it take root in you. He will give you double for your shame! I know you could use everlasting joy as well. Know that God doesn't make you feel ashamed, and He does not bring confusion your way. Get prepared to fight against the enemy by sharpening your skills in the word of God. Remember, we are victorious in Christ. You just have to walk in it.

Speak It:
- ♥ I will receive a double portion for my shame!
- ♥ I have everlasting joy!
- ♥ The joy of the Lord gives me strength!
- ♥ I have the spirit of a finisher!

Day 22

"Behold, I give unto you power to tread on serpents and scorpions, and over all the power of the enemy: and nothing shall by any means hurt you."
Luke 10:19 (KJV)

Have you ever been afraid to do something? Public speaking was my fear. I thought that the audience would laugh at my size when I was overweight. I just assumed my feelings would get hurt. My Pastor said to us one Sunday, "What would you do if you knew you couldn't fail?" When I started to think about that and this scripture, I began to look at my life and things that I wanted to do differently. This scripture also helped me with the timid spirit that I once had. Knowing that I could conquer all the power of the enemy opened my eyes to see that I should not fear meeting new people or any other situation I faced. Satan cannot harm you with any power or temptation that he tries to send your way! He has already been defeated by your Father! It's time that you realize the power that you have and that you can do anything that you put your mind to doing.

You can pursue your dreams with God's help. He gave us Holy Spirit who is our helper and our guide. In fact, I've had to listen to Him while writing this to you. If it had not been for Him, I'm 100% sure that you wouldn't be reading this today. Let this scripture sink into your heart so that you can speak it daily over anything that you think will potentially hurt you. Declare and decree it over situations at work, over issues with your children, and over any fears that you have. Nothing shall hurt you by any means! Remember, God is not like man that He should lie. Trust Him today, and move forward with confidence in Him!

Speak It:
- ♥ I have confidence in God!
- ♥ I can trample over scorpions, serpents, and over all the power of the enemy, and NOTHING shall harm me!
- ♥ I am led by Holy Spirit!
- ♥ I will accomplish all of my goals!

Day 23

"Set your affection on things above, not on things on the earth."
Colossians 3:2 (KJV)

Queen, when was the last time you monitored what you were thinking? Have you ever thought about what your thinking is devoted to each day? In order to transform and renew your mind, you must change your thoughts. The Greek-Hebrew definition of affection means "to set your mind on; be devoted to." When I was in school, my mind was set on making money upon graduation so I could take care of my children. While that was not a wrong way to think, I wasn't in the right mindset with those thoughts. My thought was that I needed to make the money. Instead, I should have been thinking that God is my provider, and He will give me opportunities to get wealth.

After I graduated, I didn't get my ideal job right away. I took one more class towards my BSN, and then I decided to focus on God just like I focused on becoming an RN. Once I passed my state test, I was not fulfilled. I thought that everything would be great once I graduated, and it wasn't. That's because I had not been consistent with putting God first in my life. There is nothing wrong with having a solid educational background, but if God is not first, you will not be fulfilled. On the other hand, when I became devoted to Him in everything, this book idea was birthed in me. When I set my mind on the things of God, rather than getting married, going out partying and drinking, or being jealous of what other people had, my life began to blossom. I was blessed with a nursing job that I desired. I even met the man of God that was destined for me, but I had to wait to be in a relationship with him.

That was a true example of setting my affections on things above and NOT on things on this earth. You know from reading my story, that I desired a relationship. Nevertheless, I had to put God first, and let it go until the appointed time. I was also able to write and publish this book because I was devoted to God. Sometimes you have to give up what you want most, to receive the gifts that God has for you. Take time to have a solid relationship with Him before you have to balance all of your earthly ones. Remember, God knows the plans that He has for you. Center your thoughts around Him, and your life will change dramatically.

Speak It:
- ♥ I set my thoughts on things above and not on things of this world!
- ♥ I wait with confidence for the things that God has for me!
- ♥ I desire His will for my life!

Day 24

"These things I have spoken unto you, that in me ye might have peace. In the world ye shall have tribulation: but be of good cheer; I have overcome the world."
John 16:33 (KJV)

I don't know about you, but I could use an abundance of peace. I like to refer to peace as when you can rest even though things are not going right in your life. It's being able to rest when you may not have enough money. It's resting when your children are not acting like they have good sense. Peace is resting while you wait for God to move on your behalf in reference to that job or that home you are waiting for. Even though we will have tribulations, storms, and difficult moments, we can rest in knowing that God overcame the world! He has defeated any and everything for you! It's time that you praise Him even when the situation is bad. Your praise confuses the enemy. His goal is to keep you down so you won't open your mouth and speak life.

Begin to speak life over every situation that is affecting your peace! Call those things that are not as though they already are. When you start doing that, you are walking in your faith. If your money is short, declare that you are a tither and God causes you to have overflow. (You better be a tither, Queen!) When you can't sleep at night, declare that you lay down and God gives you supernatural peace! Whatever it is, speak the word on it. That word will accomplish what it was sent to do. Remember, the things that we see are temporal. That means they are subject to change. Praise God in advance, for you are already an overcomer!

Speak It:
- ♥ I am an overcomer!
- ♥ I have peace in every situation!
- ♥ I speak life over myself and not death!
- ♥ I will bless the Lord, and His praises shall continually be in my mouth!

Day 25

"Thou shalt also decree a thing, and it shall be established unto thee: and the light shall shine upon thy ways."

Job 22:28 (KJV)

Your words have power, and every single word that comes out of your mouth affects your future. To decree something means "to order, command, or proclaim." (www.dictionary.com) When I had issues with my weight, I would always see myself as overweight, no matter how small I was. I had trouble losing weight that I gained during my divorce and nursing school, and I could not figure out why. I was working out, and I was trying my best to stay away from sweets. However, the weight just kept piling on more. Then, one day I realized that I kept calling myself Sherman Klump, the overweight man on The Nutty Professor. Of course, I was joking, but my words were being manifested! I was always eating, and I was gaining weight as a result. I decided to stop saying that about myself just to see what would happen. In a matter of three to four weeks, I had lost almost fifteen pounds!

Is there something going on in your life that you would like to see change? If so, pay attention to what you are speaking out of your mouth. If you are saying, "These kids are going to drive me crazy," I'm pretty sure that they are. You may think that your words don't matter, but they do. As you get more focused on this lifestyle change, you will begin to pray more with a focus and you will watch what you say! When I pray, I declare and decree what I want over my life, because I know that they will be established unto me. I am commanding them to come to me. I decree peace over your life. I decree that generational curses are broken in the name of Jesus Christ. Queen, it's time for you to speak in your God-given language, which is the language of life! From this moment forward, do not speak about your situations based on what you see. Speak what you want them to be. Remember, life and death are in the power of your tongue! If you don't have anything good to say, don't say anything at all!

Speak It:
- ♥ I speak words of life!
- ♥ I can decree a desire, and it will be established unto me!
- ♥ I am blessed and highly favored!

Day 26

"Also I say unto you, 'Whosoever shall confess me before men, him shall the Son of man also confess before the angels of God.'"

Luke 12:8 (KJV)

The Greek-Hebrew definition for confess is "to profess or acknowledge." In this verse, Jesus is talking about people confessing himself to others. Has someone ever asked you what your religion was? I know that I have been asked plenty of times. I never had trouble saying I was a Christian. However, when it came to talking about Christ, I would tend to draw back. I was not bold enough for Him. I have been blessed beyond measure, but when people would ask me how I got to certain places, I'd say, "I studied hard" or "I guess I did well on the interview." You see, I wasn't confessing Him before men. Still, the Bible tells us that if we acknowledge Him before the world, He acknowledges us before angels! I need angelic assistance, how about you?

I'm not writing this to say that God will not protect you, this is to get you out of that shell. It's easy to keep your mouth shut so you will not seem weird or be labeled as a religious freak, but that is what the devil wants. He knows that your words have power. Therefore, if we stay shy and timid with our confessions for the Lord, no one will see His grace and mercy over our lives. Queens are bold, and it's time that you speak boldly for Christ!

Whenever I get the chance to acknowledge Him, I do. If it wasn't for His love for me, I wouldn't be able to accomplish anything. It's a simple task, but we must continually acknowledge Him before this world. We cannot sit back and keep our mouths shut. I love the example that my pastor gives about sporting events. People yell and scream for their favorite teams, but can't praise God for more than thirty minutes or even raise a hand in worship. I was that person in the past. I didn't want people to laugh at how I worshiped. Now, I don't care who sees me worship. As long as God sees me, that is all that matters. Remember, as we acknowledge Him, He is doing the same for us before the angels.

Speak It:
- ♥ I confess the name of Jesus before men!
- ♥ I will stand firm on my faith in Christ!
- ♥ I am bold in Christ!

Day 27

"And we know that all things work together for good to them that love God, to them who are the called according to His purpose."
Romans 8:28 (KJV)

Do you know what your purpose is in life? If you don't know it at this current moment, it is okay. As you continue to seek God, He will give you the answers you need to move forward in your purpose. I kept hearing about purpose in church, and I was like, "I'm thirty plus years old, a mother of two, and I don't know what I am supposed to be doing." I asked my close friends, my mom, and even my mentor what they thought I was good at doing. They gave me their ideas of my purpose. Then, I asked the person who knew the answer—God. I asked Him to reveal things to me daily that I had never seen about myself, and He did just that. Do you know that if you are unsure about your purpose, you will take jobs or even move to places where you are not called to be?

I yearned for a clear understanding of who I was and what I was sent here to do. God has revealed some of those things to me. I know that you love God, and I'm sure that He has given you insights to what He wants to do in your life. I want to encourage you during this time. When you are in the process of hearing from God, it may seem that things are not going the way that you think they should. In honesty, they shouldn't. God knew who you were before you were formed in your mother's womb. The plans that He has will come to fruition in your life.

Proverbs 19:21 tells us, "It's the Lord's purpose for you that will stand." No matter what it looks like, do not lose your focus. God has already placed the POWER inside of you to manifest your purpose. All things work together for you! Trust Him and don't look to what you can make happen. God wants our faith to be completely in Him. Your Father is supernatural, and what He will do is far above anything you can imagine!

Speak It:
- ♥ All things work together for my good!
- ♥ I am called according to God's purpose!
- ♥ I have the power to complete my God-given assignments!

Day 28

"For I am persuaded, that neither death, nor life, nor angels, nor principalities, nor powers, nor things present, nor things to come, nor height, nor depth, nor any other creature, shall be able to separate us from the love of God, which is in Christ Jesus our Lord."
Romans 8:38-39 (KJV)

Every now and then, I would have what my girlfriends and I call "moments." A moment is when you have a flashback of your past or feel pressure in reference to future goals. You may become angry about a relationship that didn't work. It could be because you still have desires to be in a relationship, when God is really trying to work on you at the moment. It could even just be a day of condemnation. You might think about the abortion, the divorce, the job you lost, or that you just are not where you thought you would be at this particular time in your life. These thoughts would make us feel that we were unloved by God, and that definitely is not true.

I believe that those moments are times when our flesh is in need of something that God is purging us from. He is trying to get our focus back on Him and into our true identity in Him. I would get angry when I had those moments, because they came so often. I would think to myself, "I'm not moving forward. These emotions are setting me back. I won't get to where God wants me to be." However, I was completely wrong. Every time I had those moments, He was right there. He held my hand

and let me know that the flashbacks were just a part of the process. In actuality, I became stronger every time I had those moments. I knew how to fight against them with the scriptures that were now embedded in my soul. As a result, I became the woman of God that I was always destined to be. This can also work for you!

As you continue to read this devotional, know that nothing can keep God's heart from you. Nothing that you have done, said, or will do will stop Him from loving you. This love will overflow you with peace, gratitude, and a worship for God that no one else will understand. When you have those moments, just remember that you are being molded by the best carpenter in the history of the world! The Bible says in Isaiah 61:3, "You will be given beauty for your ashes, the oil of joy for mourning, and the garment of praise for the spirit of heaviness." Enjoy the process, Queen. The end result will blow your mind!

Speak It:
- ♥ Nothing can separate me from the love of God!
- ♥ I am equipped with everything that I need in Christ!
- ♥ Patience is having her perfect work!

Day 29

"Jesus said, "The first in importance is, Listen, Israel: The Lord your God is one; So love the Lord God with all your passion and prayer and intelligence and energy!""
Mark 12:30 (MSG)

Love is a strong word that some people often misuse. After many experiences with what I thought was love, I don't think I was ever in love or that I loved properly. With this realization, I started to think about my relationship with Christ. I had placed Him on the backseat or sometimes somewhere on a shelf when I was of the world. I gave Him second place when a man came into my life speaking words that I craved and longed to hear. We are reminded in this scripture that we should love Him with all of our passion. I have always been passionate about school. I would be very organized, and I stayed up all hours of the night studying. However, I never put effort into my love for Christ. After many heartaches, unnecessary relationships, and drama, I knew that I needed to love Him with everything I had within me.

Wherever you are right now in your walk with Christ, I need you to dig a little deeper. If you pray only in the shower, try setting aside at least twenty extra minutes a day with God in prayer. If you only read a daily scripture on your phone, try to pick up your Bible and read the whole chapter. Time goes by extremely fast, and we must dedicate it to the most important relationship we will ever have. God loved us so much that He gave His only son. I don't know about you, but I wouldn't give my children up for anyone—especially knowing that they wouldn't cherish the relationship and wouldn't listen to me! God, Jesus Christ, and Holy Spirit show us a perfect example of real love. As you move forward with this journey, passionately love Him. When you are frustrated with a human relationship, use the energy towards growing deeper with God. If you worked hard for that degree, use those study skills to get into His word. He will birth things in you that you never knew were possible when you truly start loving Him. Remember, what you need is already in you. It's time that you trust God and walk by faith.

Speak It:
- ♥ I will love God with all my heart, soul, mind, and strength!
- ♥ God has already placed everything I need within me!
- ♥ I walk by faith and not by sight!

Day 30

> *"Create in me a clean heart, O God; and renew a right spirit within me."*
>
> Psalms 51:10 (KJV)

In this scripture, a clean heart is defined as something pure and genuine. In the Old Testament, the Greek word for *clean* (tahowr) is used to describe things that were pure and capable of being used. Over the past thirty days, God has begun to do a new thing in you. If you are anything like I was, your heart may be in many pieces. My spirit was broken in more ways than one, and I could barely get through a day without thinking about how someone had hurt me at some point in my life. I thought every man was lying to me, even when God had spoken truth to me through Holy Spirit. I needed a renewing of my spirit, and God has given me just that. He will do the same for YOU!

Queens, we need to be vessels that God can use. For that to happen, we must surrender to Him. There may be some things, people, or even television shows that you need to give up in order to get closer to Him during this time of transformation. Your spirit is fed by what you listen to and what you watch. Take a moment to think about what subtle messages you are allowing to creep into your spirit. Are they things of good or things of drama? Do they display sexual immorality or negative images? Dedicate this time to God so that He can clean and mend your heart. Let Him purge unwanted things out of your spirit and make you anew. God wants to fix all of your broken areas; He just needs you to present them to Him. This devotional will not only help you get into His word, but it will also help save your spiritual life like it did for me while I was writing it. Let this be the last day that you are frustrated about life. Over the next thirty-five days make living for Christ a lifestyle and not just something you do on Sunday, Christmas, and Easter.

Speak It:
- ♥ I give all of my broken pieces to Christ!
- ♥ Through Christ, I am made new!
- ♥ My heart is made new in Christ!

Day 31

"Trust in the Lord with all thine heart; and lean not unto thine own understanding. In all thy ways acknowledge him and he will direct thy paths."
Proverbs 3:5-6 (KJV)

Do you often make wrong choices? Do you take jobs or offers that seem good, but then it turns out to be the worst decision you've ever made? If so, I'm pretty positive that you did not trust God enough to acknowledge Him so that He could direct you. Usually when you trust someone, you are confident that what they tell you is beneficial for you. You listen to their advice, and if they suggest something, you easily agree and accept it. You may seek input from this person when you have a big decision to make, and their response may even affect your decision. This is how you should put your trust in God. You should not make decisions based on what you can see or understand. With every single step you take, you must first get the opinion of Holy Spirit.

If you don't currently acknowledge God before you make any decisions, I am asking you to evaluate your relationship with Him right now. The most amazing thing about our Father is that He is so merciful and forgiving. No matter how many times we mess up, He is right there with His hand out ready to brush our knees off and tell us to give it another try! He wants you to trust Him. Furthermore, He wants you to seek Him before you make any decisions. If you can trust a mentor or accountability partner, why can't you give the One who knows the plans that He has for you 100% of your trust? It was hard for me to think about acknowledging Him before I made any decisions. However, once I got tired of making the wrongs ones, I didn't want to use my limited or anxious thinking anymore. So I threw my hands up in surrender! In order to have the transformation that the word of God can bring into your life, you must acknowledge Him and trust that He will direct your path. Choose to start right now. Trust and lean on Him, and He will direct you.

Speak It:
- I trust in the Lord with all my heart!
- I acknowledge the Lord first, and He directs my path!
- I have patience to wait on an answer from God!

Day 32

"And he said unto me, My grace is sufficient for thee: for my strength is made perfect in weakness. Most gladly therefore will I rather glory in my infirmities that the power of Christ may rest upon me."

2 Corinthians 12:9 (KJV)

Once during a time of corporate fasting, I decided to give up talking to a male that I was growing close to romantically. We both knew that we needed to grow before entering a relationship, and a corporate fast was the best time to work on this. In the beginning, it seemed to be a horrible mistake to choose to fast from him. I wanted to hear his voice and hear him tell me that he loved the woman I was, but then God revealed something to me in my moment of weakness. I didn't know it at the time, but letting go of a fleshly man would bring me closer to the One that I needed the most. During my emotional moments, God showed me that He loved me first. He made it clear to me that that I am the first thing on His mind when He wakes me up in the morning!

Everything that I was seeking from an earthly man God already was. I just never took the time to focus completely on Him. You may need strength in other areas, but I needed an emotional miracle. I had so many unhealthy relationships that I would hold on to for dear life thinking I would lose them. In reality, they needed to be lost. However, when God speaks to you about your future, it's hard to let go of something that you have desired for so long. God's grace made me strong during my weak moments. I was able to get through the fast without communicating prematurely. Your struggle may be different. You may need to stop smoking, drinking, or hanging out in bars and clubs. Those things may be sore spots for you, but I am here to let you know that you must run to God in your weak moments. You must pray to Him, and He will get you through. If you fall, it's okay. God is there to pick you up and start all over again. You must realize that He is there making you stronger than ever in your weakest moments. Push forward into your purpose and destiny in Christ. I promise He will not disappoint you.

Speak It:
- When I am weak, God's grace is sufficient and makes me strong!
- I am an overcomer!
- I let God lead me into my purpose and destiny!

Day 33

"For I know the thoughts that I think toward you, saith the Lord, thoughts of peace and not of evil, to give you an expected end."
Jeremiah 29:11 (KJV)

When I first started really hearing from God, it was hard for me to believe the things that He was saying. I was so accustomed to bad things happening in my life that I couldn't even fathom that things would happen for me as He said. I didn't believe that they would happen as fast or even that I deserved these blessings. I had to really meditate and say this verse out loud to myself daily to rid myself of the negative thoughts that were coming to me. God's plans for us are for peace, which means that nothing will be missing, lacking, or broken. He wants us completely whole! He knows that nothing He has destined for us includes evil. Therefore, any adversity or affliction is not from Him.

We may have obstacles, but we can overcome anything with His help because He has already defeated Satan on our behalf. He knows our future, and it is more abundant than you or I could ever dream. Think of the biggest plan that you have for yourself, and then triple it! God is so awesome that He would and can do that for you. As you are getting closer to God and hearing His voice, I encourage you to receive His plans with a cheerful heart. Do not condemn yourself. He loves you, and He only wants peace to abound towards you. Let Him speak to you, and believe what He says! He has your best interest at heart. No matter what you have done, nothing can separate you from His love. NOTHING!

Speak It:
- ♥ God knows the plans that He has for me—thoughts of peace and not of evil!
- ♥ I will openly accept God's love!
- ♥ I am spotless and blameless in His sight!

Day 34

"For I [Myself] will give you a mouth and such utterance and wisdom that all of your foes combined will be unable to stand against or refute."

Luke 21:15 (AMP)

Have you ever been in a situation when all the odds were against you? Have you ever thought that you weren't good enough for a position? Maybe you thought that you didn't fit in with certain people because of their background, but you were in their midst anyway. You may have "haters" that just don't like you no matter what you do. Sometimes your purpose will place you in front of people who may have more degrees, money, and influence in certain arenas, BUT the God you serve is much greater! I need you to know that you don't ever have to back down from an opportunity to speak for Him. Whenever you get the chance to educate or influence someone or a group of people, make sure you have no fear. Do not be moved by the name of the organization, the people who are in the room, or that it may be your first time speaking. He will give you wisdom, and no one will be able to come against the truth.

This also holds true as it relates issues that involve the court system. You must always speak out of your mouth what you desire, NOT what it looks like. I have heard many stories of how things could have gone wrong, and the Christian individual was blessed by the outcome. No matter what the lawyer says, you speak faith-filled words, and God will honor you. He gets glory when our prayers are answered. So please do not think that your Father does not want to see you victorious in Him. From this moment on, believe that God will always give you utterance and wisdom in every situation that you face. Start walking in faith, and watch Him transform your life!

Speak It:
- ♥ I speak with God's wisdom!
- ♥ I only speak faith-filled words!
- ♥ Greater is He that is in me, than he that is in this world!

Day 35

"This I say then, Walk in the Spirit, and ye shall not fulfil the lust of the flesh."

Galatians 5:16 (KJV)

Communicating with and through Holy Spirit is one aspect of my walk in Christ that has helped me. I used to listen to people talk about hearing from God daily, and I was like, "I don't hear from Him at all!" Well, once I got hungry and thirsty for the things of God, I started hearing Him clearly. When we walk in the spirit, our flesh gets weaker and weaker. However, each day that you seek God, He will build you up more and more. It will become easier to refuse fleshly activities that have you confused, sick, or hurt. Your mind won't be as cluttered, and you will be able to hear from God more. The Bible tells us that Holy Spirit is our helper, guide, intercessor, counselor, and strengthener, to name a few. I'm sure those things are needed in your life daily. You must remember that we can and must have a relationship with Holy Spirit.

When Jesus died for us, He let us know that Holy Spirit would be coming after Him. Therefore, it is essential that we have a relationship with Him. I encourage you to take time each day to commune with Holy Spirit. He can assist you with walking in the Spirit so that you will not fulfill the lust of the flesh. Be aware that as you seek this relationship, you will have to fight for it! The enemy of your soul does not want you to know your true identity. He knows that your identity is revealed when you seek after Christ and have a relationship with Holy Spirit. Do not quit! When you pray, let Holy Spirit know that He is welcome, and He will come to you. Make a commitment today to be Holy Spirit led.

    Speak It:
- I walk in the Spirit and not in the flesh!
- Holy Spirit is my helper and my guide!
- I have a listening ear to Holy Spirit!

Day 36

"There hath no temptation taken you but such as is common to man: but God is faithful, who will not suffer you to be tempted above that ye are able; but will with the temptation also make a way to escape, that ye may be able to bear it."
1 Corinthians 10:13 (KJV)

Have you ever felt like you were suffocating emotionally? I know that you have heard the saying, "God will not put more on you than you can bear." There will be times in your Christian walk where you have trials, and you will be tempted. Nevertheless, God will always provide a way for you to overcome any situation. I thought that I wasn't going to be able to make it when I was going through the rough time in my first marriage. No matter what I did, I couldn't fix the situation. I was happy one minute and sad the next. I wanted to be married, then I wanted a divorce. Confusion was my daily companion, but God was still with me during that time. My escape was right in His arms. It didn't happen overnight because I was not accustomed to love or even to loving a man that I could not see. I rebelled and ran for a while. Though, God got my undivided attention in the end just as He wanted.

If you are going through a storm, test, or trial in your life, I'm telling you to stay strong! You may be tempted to quit, but that is not an option for you. You are of a royal priesthood, and your father defeated the enemy on your behalf even before you were born. Cry out to Him for His help. Cry out to Holy Spirit to comfort and guide you. Most importantly, worship your Heavenly Father for being who He is. Your praise confuses the enemy. It will seem foreign to you and uncomfortable for a little while. However, if you yield to Holy Spirit, you will be able to bear any situation that tries to tempt you. Furthermore, you will put on a garment of praise for your mourning!

Speak It:
- ♥ God will provide me with a way of escape!
- ♥ I am victorious in Christ!
- ♥ Nothing shall harm me by any means!

Day 37

> *"Delight thyself also in the Lord; and He shall give thee the desires of thine heart."*
>
> Psalms 37:4 (KJV)

The word *delight* means "to please (someone) greatly." (www.dictionary.com) Before I was really serious about Christ, I would quote this scripture often. I was still bound by my flesh. Consequently, I thought that if I attended church and paid my tithes, I would be delighting myself in Him. I was absolutely wrong. Hebrews 11:6 lets us know that without faith, it's impossible to please God. How is your faith in God at this current moment? Do you worry a lot? Do you give God your tithe and let Him pour out blessings for you, or do you work endless hours of overtime and foolishly spend the money?

Faith in God means that we rely solely on Him. I remember my mother always saying that God was her source. It was not any job that she had but God! I realized that as I grew in my walk with Christ, He was the one who even woke me up to go to the job! In fact, He is the reason that I even was offered the job! When you have faith in God, it completely changes your mindset. You will realize that you don't have to be intimidated by upper management. You will come to the knowledge that you set the tone in your work place. Do you know how you do that? It happens when you do what pleases your Father. Faith comes by hearing and hearing by the word of God.

When I started to get more into His word (besides Sundays), I became more confident. With this confidence and newfound knowledge from the word, I began to see His genuine love for me. This increased my faith and gave me a hunger and thirst for more! That was the beginning of my delight in Him. You will get to a point where you will miss not communicating in prayer with your Father. You will seek time just to listen and be still in His presence, because it is so comforting! You find rest when you delight yourself in Him. Once that is your desire, He will do exceedingly and abundantly above all that you can ask, think, or imagine! Your desires will be met times one thousand! I urge you to seek Him, not to get something tangible, but seek Him to be filled with the overflow of His love for you. That sweet place in Christ will keep you hungry for His presence daily.

Speak It:
- ♥ I delight myself in the Lord daily!
- ♥ I seek after Christ with my whole heart!
- ♥ I have faith that pleases God!

Day 38

"But seek ye first the kingdom of God, and his righteousness; and all these things will be added unto you. Take therefore no thought for the morrow: for the morrow shall take thought for the things of itself. Sufficient unto the day is the evil thereof."
Matthew 6:33-34 (KJV)

What is the first thing you do when you get up in the morning? Some may go to the bathroom or brush their teeth. When I worked the overnight shift, my time was really messed up. As a result, I never really had a good sleep pattern. Therefore, my mornings would begin in the afternoon. When I had days off, I would try to get up and pray or even read the Bible in the mornings. However, I continually hit the snooze button! During a time of fasting with my church, I decided that I was going to seek God with everything in me. I made it a point to go to bed early when I had a night off, so that I could pray before my family started their day. Yes, I did hit the snooze button a time or two or three, but I got up and sought Him first. As I began to seek Him before checking my phone for text messages, emails, or game notifications, He began to speak to me in a way that was shocking. Just the fact that I could hear Him clearly was new to me! When I worked overnight and didn't pray, I would literally feel different. I missed the communication with the One who knew me better than even my own momma! I needed that time in prayer and meditation in the word.

One thing that I desired was to be able to take care of my children without my mother's help. Financially, I wanted to pay all the bills and not have to split anything. I felt that my children were not her responsibility. She was always willing to help, but it was a desire of my heart. While seeking God, He would let me know that my children would be taken care of no matter what. As I began to have an ear for His voice, the worrying stopped. I realized that I was worthy of His love even when I didn't feel like it. In addition, I began to enjoy each day for itself. I didn't worry about tomorrow, tuition for school, buying food, or what activities I could afford. I listened to Him, and all of my needs were met emotionally, spiritually, mentally, and physically. I cannot stress enough the importance of going into God's presence daily. Talk to Him before you tell your problems to someone who can't help you, even when you don't feel like it! Trust me, there will be days when your flesh doesn't feel like praying, but press anyway. God is not like us. He cannot lie. His word says what is true. Get into it and seek Him. In return, all you need will be added.

Speak It:
- ♥ I seek first the kingdom of God!
- ♥ I consult with God before anyone else!
- ♥ I do not worry about anything!

Day 39

"Let you conversation be without covetousness; and be content with such things as ye have: for he hath said, I will never leave thee, nor forsake thee."
Hebrews 13:5 (KJV)

Do you often think about why other people have what you want? Are you jealous of people who are getting married, receiving a new job, or just even in a new relationship? If this is your mindset, I understand. I have been there before. I would even get jealous of close friends because I wanted a relationship or a secure job that would allow me to be on my own with my children. As I started to walk more closely with God, my request to Him was to make me content with what I already had. I wanted to enjoy my children without a husband. I wanted to live life as a single woman with no regrets. Realizing that what God has for Geneva is for Geneva, made me understand that I can't have what other people have! I also learned that I didn't want their life anyway!

God knows the plans that He has for you and only you. There is no need to covet or be jealous of what other people have. If you look at the situation and remove your emotions, which are temporary, you will see the truth. When you get frustrated with your life, do not desire someone else's life or blessings. Trust and know that God is always with you. He knows your desires and needs. Be content with everything you have at this current moment, and continue to seek God. Do not look at what others are doing. Instead, focus on God. If you follow His direction, you will always be content. If you have a question, ask Him. He is there, and it is time that you realize that He WILL speak back to you.

Speak It:
- ♥ God will never leave me nor forsake me!
- ♥ I do not covet the things of others!
- ♥ What God has for _____ (Insert Name) is for _____ (Insert Name).

Day 40

"But ye are a chosen generation, a royal priesthood, a holy nation, a peculiar people, that ye should shew forth the praises of him who hath called you out of darkness in his marvelous light."
1 Peter 2:9 (KJV)

One thing many new or young Christians lack is knowing their identity. I never knew that I was supposed to stand out or be different. Whether it was because I talked different or because of my mindset, I was supposed to stand out. Sometimes, we just think that we should be doing what the crowd is doing. On the contrary, God has chosen each and every one of us before we were in our mothers' wombs. You are royalty! Did you know that? You are peculiar, which means that you belong exclusively to God. Do you declare or make widely known that Jesus has brought you out or saved you? Are you a closet Christian?

I was not the person in this scripture until I surrendered to His will for me. To shew forth means to declare and make known widely. You don't necessarily have to be on television preaching, but you should be telling people about how you became free. Tell them why you are so full of joy and peace. When your mindset begins to shift, you will act differently and you will look different too! You must grab a hold of this identity NOW! Walk with your head held high, and have confidence knowing that God chose you first! No matter what you have been through or what is coming, you will get through it and be victorious in the end. Moreover, after each test or trial, do not be ashamed to give your testimony. That is what you are supposed to do! Be bold in and for Christ!

Speak It:
- ♥ I am chosen by God!
- ♥ I am of a royal priesthood!
- ♥ I belong exclusively to Christ!

Day 41

"And the Lord shall make thee the head, and not the tail; and thou shalt be above only, and thou shalt not be beneath; if that thou hearken unto the commandments of the Lord thy God, which I command thee this day to observe and do them."

Deuteronomy 28:13 (KJV)

I know that one hundred percent of the Christian population knows or can recite the first part of this scripture! I'm also pretty sure that you didn't know that it had an if after it! One of the most important things that I have learned while seeking God is that I cannot serve two masters. I thought it was okay to hang out in clubs because I love music. What I realized is that I couldn't party until 3 A.M. and make it to church on time every weekend. Subsequently, I started to stay home more and more. Partying became my outlet, instead of God and His word. The scripture tells us that we will be the head and not the tail, above only and not beneath, BUT we must do what God commands. He delights in answering our prayers, because those answers give Him glory.

You have to remember to surrender to Him daily. Your life shouldn't be your own. You shouldn't just do what you want. Did you know that? You must be led by Holy Spirit. Observe what the word of God says, and do it! Let me be clear. God's love for you is never-ending. If you slip up, He's not going to give up on you. However, just do not think that you can "do" church on Sunday, and then live anyway you want Monday through

Saturday. Your Christian walk and relationship with God should be a lifestyle. Make a choice right now to stay committed. Be steadfast and hold on to the promises of God. He wants to bless you, but do not take advantage of God's mercy and grace that is renewed every morning. Surrender to Him and watch for your overflow of blessings.

Speak It:
- ♥ I am the head and not the tail!
- ♥ I am above only and not beneath!
- ♥ I am a follower of God's commandments!

Day 42

"If your first concern is to look after yourself, you'll never find yourself. But if you forget about yourself and look to me, you'll find both yourself and me."
                                        Matthew 10:39 (MSG)

    Surrender is a key in transformation. Sometimes you don't want to let go. You may not want to learn something new or think "outside of the box." Nonetheless, He will lead you when you forget about how uncomfortable, awkward, or how shy you may feel, and look to God to make you bold and confident in Him. I've had issues with men that led me not to trust them. Accordingly, I would rely on myself to make things happen. I was only concerned with looking after me and my children. Yes, I loved God, but like I've mentioned before, I didn't seek Him. As a result, I didn't know who I was or who I could be through Him. In essence, I was lost and surrendering was the only option I had left. Being hurt, sad, depressed, confused, and every other negative emotion was too much for me. I knew that I was a child of the Most High God, but I didn't feel like it! I asked God to take away the desires that were literally killing me from the inside out. I needed Him to take away the wants to be with someone who was no good for me. I begged Him to take them away, and our Father, being the great God that He is, did just that!
    As I continued to pray, seek Him, and read books about Holy Spirit, prayer, and fasting, my eyes were opened to a life that I saw in my dreams. When I forgot

about myself and MY desires, I was able to see what I needed. I saw myself as a daughter of a King, which made me a Queen. It's time for you to look to God so that you can find yourself and find out who He is and who He wants to be in your life! If you don't know Christ, you really don't know yourself. Realize, Queen, that you were born for a reason. There is someone on this earth that you were born to help. You were not intended just to receive a husband or to be a mom. God may need you to heal someone. This book may be a healing tool for you. Think about that, and then forget about yourself. When you find Him, you will find the person you were created to be!

Speak It:
- ♥ I am the daughter of the Most High God!
- ♥ I give myself to God!
- ♥ I am His beloved!

Day 43

"Enter ye in at the strait gate: for wide is the gate, and broad is the way, that leadeth to destruction, and many there be which go thereat: Because strait is the gate, and narrow is the way, which leadeth unto life, and few there be that find it."
Matthew 7:13-14 (KJV)

One question I like to ask people is: "What ya life like?" Yes, I ask the question exactly like that—grammatically incorrect. ☺ If you ask yourself this question, it will let you know which path you are on right now. For a long time, I chose the wide gate, and I did what everyone else was doing. I partied a lot, I got drunk, I had children out of wedlock, and I was still professing that I was a Christian. If you've had any of these situations arise in your life, I'm not saying that it disqualifies you from Christianity. What I want you to see is that this wide gate led me to emotional destruction. I was lonely, needy, and battled with depression. Christianity should be your lifestyle. Yes, it does seem easier to do all of the fun or "worldly" things. This scripture is letting us know that many people choose the wide gate. This gate would be considered the in-crowd or what everyone else is doing. It also clearly states that this way is going to lead you to destruction!

Please don't be like the old Geneva and worry about what everyone else is doing. It's none of your business! Share Christ with them, and choose the straight and narrow path that leads unto life. You are God's chosen one, and you belong exclusively unto Him! Stop thinking you must fit in with the crowd. That is a lie! You are meant to stand out based on the light that exudes from you. There will be few people who are living like you, and that's okay. You just keep living for God. Keep giving your testimony. Keep studying His word. He is a rewarder of those that diligently seek Him. So open your eyes to the truth, and it will lead you into a long, prosperous life in Him. It is the deception of the devil that keeps us bound and keeps us wanting to live for ourselves and not for God. It's time for you to turn down the things you desire, and seek God to see if your desires match up with His. Once they match up with His will, your life will be much more peaceful.

Speak It:
- ♥ I choose life!
- ♥ I follow the straight path in Christ Jesus!
- ♥ I seek God and know that He is my rewarder!

Day 44

"Whosoever cometh to me; and hearth my sayings, and doeth them, I will shew you to whom he is like: He is like a man which built an house and digged deep, and laid the foundation on a rock: and when the flood arose, the steam beat vehemently upon that house, and could not shake it: for it was founded upon a rock. But he that hearth, and doeth not, is like a man that without a foundation built a house upon the earth; against which the stream did beat vehemently, and immediately it fell; and the ruin of that house was great."

Luke 6:47-49 (KJV)

It is extremely important that you have a solid foundation in Christ. I know that you have heard people say, "When it rains it pours." That may be true for them. However, with a solid foundation, you do not have to be swept away when the flood comes! In order to have this solid foundation in Christ, you must do three things.

First, you need to come to Him. Commit yourself and your whole being to Him. When I decided to come to Christ fully, it wasn't easy. My flesh didn't want to submit, but I was tired of the frustration. I was frustrated because I was trying to fix the situations myself rather than giving them over to Him. You cannot fight battles on your own or in your human strength. When you come to Him remove yourself, and let Him take control.

The second thing you need to do is hear His sayings. Read His word daily! If you desire to hear from Him, you must know what His word says. When you know the word, you're able to decipher what is His voice and what is not.

Lastly, you need to do what He says! It's great to come and hear what He says. Though, if you don't follow His directions, then you will be like the house with no foundation. As soon as a storm comes, you will fall immediately and come to great ruin. If you are reading this, I am sure that you've already had some storms come in your life that may have seemed like they were sent to destroy you.

The great thing about being a child of a King is that He gives us answers to every question that we have. Still, you must come, hear, and do what He tells you. Disobedience essentially means that you don't have faith in God. You don't believe what He said in His word. Without faith, it is impossible to please God! It's time that you choose Him instead of walking in your natural abilities. A house with a solid foundation is unshakeable! When the storms try to come at you in the future, you will have the word inside you to combat them! It's time to be steadfast and keep walking towards transformation. Christ is the solid rock, Beloved, stand on Him!

Speak It:
- ♥ I am a doer of the Word of God!
- ♥ In Christ, I have a solid foundation!
- ♥ I listen and follow Christ's instructions!

Day 45

"Come unto me, all ye that labour and are heavy laden, and I will give you rest."
                                   Matthew 11:28 (KJV)

Labour, in this instance, is referring to spiritual anxieties. I already mentioned that I struggled with a need for love. This anxiety caused me much torment. My spirit was very heavy at certain points in my life. Even during this writing process, I had to give my spiritual anxieties to Him. My mind was racing. I always thought about how I could make things happen. I worried about who I needed to hold on to, just so I could see with my natural eye what they were doing. True faith is not seeing with our natural eye. True faith is saying your house is paid for when you've only made your first mortgage payment. You may not see it yet, but it's coming! Giving my anxieties to Christ led me to a true place of worship. We are to worship God in spirit and in truth.

How can you worship with anxieties boggling your spirit? Did you know that there are things going on in the spiritual realm at all times? When we walk by faith, we use our spiritual eyes and let God do the work. No longer are you anxious about love. No longer are you anxious about finances. No longer do you fear your future. You know that your Heavenly Father knows your expected end. No matter what today looks like, you can go to Him, and He will give you rest. My desire for you, Beloved, is that God gives you peace that surpasses all understanding in every area of your life. Continue daily to come to Him in prayer and give Him all of your anxieties. His word does not return void. He will give you rest when you give your anxieties Him.

Speak It:
- ♥ I cast all my anxieties on God!
- ♥ I find sweet rest in His presence!
- ♥ I have peace that surpasses my understanding!

Day 46

"For if ye live after the flesh, ye shall die: but if ye through the Spirit do mortify the deeds of the body, ye shall live."

Romans 8:13 (KJV)

    Throughout this journey of writing, I have realized that I need Holy Spirit more now than ever before. When you seriously make a decision to live for Christ, you must turn down what you want in exchange for His will for your life. The only way to do this is with the help of Holy Spirit. If I had lived after my flesh, you would not be reading this right now. I would have never stepped out in faith and let Him lead me. My dream and my purpose could potentially be dead right now, but I pushed passed the tiredness. I pushed pass the thoughts of doubt, and I let Holy Spirit comfort me and be my guide. Everything that I had done before this time of surrender to Christ was done under a fleshly desire. I chose what Geneva wanted, and I was killing myself slowly.

    It's time that you yield to Holy Spirit. Now, I will warn you that He is not going to force you to do anything. You have to make a conscious effort to seek after Him on your own. Once you step out and let Him know that you are willing, He will be right there to hold your hand. I gave up my desire for a relationship while writing this devotional. I had to focus and be in tune with my purpose. It wasn't easy, but look at the outcome. I fasted and gave up my plate so that my spirit man could be stronger and could withstand any attack the devil thought would stop me. I encourage you to yield today. Moreover, I encourage you to continue to grow your relationship with Holy Spirit as you read the word of God. You will have all the power to live a prosperous life if you yield today!

Speak It:
- ♥ I walk after the Spirit and not the flesh!
- ♥ My Spirit is getting stronger each day!
- ♥ I sacrifice my will for the will of God!

Day 47

> "What shall we then say to these things?
> If God be for us, who can be against us? "
> Romans 8:31(KJV)

In the previous verses of Romans 8, we are given insight on how life is with Holy Spirit. As you continue to make the decision to yield, your mindset should be changing. When you begin to wrap your mind around who you are in Christ, nothing will be able to stop you! When you are led by the Spirit, it qualifies you to be a child of God. Since you have that same spirit inside of you that overcame the world, why are you afraid of tomorrow? He knows your expected end, and it's a great one! I will keep reminding you that your Father is supernatural. Let go of this worldly vision of life. Stop looking at how much things cost, where the war is starting, and what virus is coming into your area. God is for you! Nothing can be against you!

When you walk in the Spirit and you listen to His directives, you are being led by Christ. One thing you have to be watchful of is your mouth. Out of the heart, the mouth speaks. You may be going through some things right now that have you thinking opposite of what the Word of God says. Still, I am begging you to put a lid on that mouth of yours. If your words do not speak faith, keep quiet! If you don't have anything good to say, you can even quote this scripture. *If God be for me, who can be against me?* Say it even when you don't feel anything. Your feelings are temporary anyway, and they can change at a moment's notice. So can your situation when God is involved. Look forward to today knowing that God is on your side and nothing can stop you.

Speak It:
- ♥ If God be for me, no one can be against me!
- ♥ I speak faith-filled words!
- ♥ I will continue to walk by Faith and not by sight!

Day 48

"If ye have faith as a grain of mustard seed, ye shall say unto this mountain, Remove hence to yonder place; and it shall remove; and nothing shall be impossible unto you."
                                               Matthew 17:20 (KJV)

    While becoming a more mature woman of God, I have learned that my words MUST always line up with what God has promised about my life. Faith sometimes can make you look like you are crazy. At times in my journey, I have even felt crazy. Yet, those feelings were always temporary. Is there something that is consistently a mountain in your life? My mountain was that of relationships. As I mentioned earlier, I yearned for them—especially with men. During the process of writing this devotional, I had to give this mountain to God a couple of times. It was so heavy in my spirit, and I did not know why. The one thing that opened up that window of breakthrough for me was that I said every day, "Satan I am walking by Faith, and this mountain has been removed!" Now, I could have just cried for ten minutes or had a whole conversation with myself on how I should give up and not wait on God, BUT my spirit was stronger than my flesh!

    When you give your mountains to God, He will take them. However, there may be a daily release that you have to do until it is settled in your spirit that nothing is impossible with that mustard seed-sized faith. Eventually, your faith will get stronger, but we must conquer the small mountains first. When I was struggling with my mountain, I stopped writing, and I was almost defeated. Yet, when I look at the end product of this devotional, I know that it was all for you! No matter what you are going through, don't give up. DO NOT GIVE UP! The enemy of your soul would love for you to throw in the towel and do what everyone else is doing. Satan would love for you to think that you can't live life the way God has destined for you to live. Do not fall for his lies! Your purpose will help someone else overcome! Put your faith muscles to work today, and let God use you. You were born for a purpose, and it's time that you listen to Holy Spirit's direction and walk in it. Yes, some days may seem harder than others, but we are always victorious in Christ. Nothing is impossible to you when you are led by Him!

Speak It:
- ♥ I have mountain moving faith!
- ♥ Nothing is impossible with Christ!
- ♥ I speak to my mountains, and they are removed!

Day 49

> *"Bring ye all the tithes into the storehouse, that there may be meat in mine house, and prove me now herewith, saith the Lord of hosts, if I will not open you the windows of heaven, and pour you out a blessing, that there shall not be room enough to receive it. And I will rebuke the devourer for your sakes, and he shall not destroy the fruits of your ground; neither shall your vine cast her fruit before the time in the field, saith the Lord of hosts."*
>
> Malachi 3:10-11 (KJV)

I know that you may be wondering why this verse is in a devotional. Well, I had to add this one in because of the prosperity aspect. I have always been a tither, whether the income came from a summer job or a full time job. I saw my mother tithe, and even though I didn't really know the benefits, I did it anyway. As I grew in the things of God, it became clear to me that some of the blessings that I received in the past were from my tithing. I know that people get all caught up in who the pastor is and what he is doing with the money, but I encourage you not to look at it that way. The ten percent that I am giving back to the church is not to my pastor. I am giving that unto God. Our pastors don't rebuke the devourer for our sake or open up the windows of heaven. They are just a vessel to get the word to us.

Are there areas in your life where you are lacking? If so, I think it's time that you check your tithes. If you are a tither, keep on going. Even when it seems like you could use the money for something else, don't! God sees your obedience, and He will bless you. Since God decided to bless us with another day on this earth, and we have the ability to go to work, I don't understand why is it such a battle to give back a small percentage. If you are in a position where you think that you cannot afford to pay your tithes, I encourage you to have faith in God. I look at it in this manner, I waste ten percent or more of my pay when I eat out. You may have a daily love affair with WaWa or Starbucks. Does that equal the ten percent you should be giving to God? Maybe you smoke cigarettes. Whatever it is that you can do without, let it go. Even as a single mother, the first thing I do when I get paid is give God His ten percent. I don't second guess it or hesitate. We've never been homeless or hungry; God has always made a way for us even when our money was low. He will make a way for you too! Make a decision today to give ten percent back to God the next time you are blessed to receive your earnings from work. Give with a cheerful heart, and do not hesitate! Just step out on faith, Beloved, when that window opens, you won't have room enough to store it!

Speak It:
- ♥ I am a tither, and God will pour out a blessing so big that I will not have room enough to store it!
- ♥ I am a tither, and God rebukes the devourer for my sake!
- ♥ I am a cheerful giver!

Day 50

"Cast the burden upon the Lord, and He shall sustain thee: he shall never suffer the righteous to be moved."
Psalms 55:22 (KJV)

    I am sure that something has weighed you down at one time or another. It could have been the stresses of school, family, friends, or just daily life events. Those things that were weighing you down can be defined as burdens. I've had one burden in particular that I had to continually give to God, until I realized that I was letting the enemy of my soul have rule over my mind. I also had to let go of the guilt of having my children out of wedlock and bringing them into a situation where they wouldn't see their fathers the way I would've liked them to. When I was tired or overwhelmed with being a single mother, I would constantly beat myself up. The main thing that I was burdened by was the financial responsibility. However, I was still a tither during that time, and the Bible clearly tells me that God will rebuke the devourer for my sake and that He will open up a window and pour me out a blessing that I wouldn't have room enough to store. I knew this, and I quoted this verse, but I still was burdened. It was not until I began writing this to you that I took my thoughts back!

    I know without a shadow of a doubt that the Lord will sustain me. He will strengthen me and give me the ability to make it through what I think are hard times. You know what, Beloved? He can and will do the same thing for you daily. Every day has its own worries. I am now living in this current moment. I know that my future with Christ has victory in it, because He has overcome the world for both you and I. Whatever is going on in your life, know that He will give you strength to get through. When you have the word of God inside of you, it will come to your remembrance at the exact time that you need it. During this journey of discovering your true identity in Christ, it's most important that you get into His word. The enemy of your soul attacks you in your thoughts, but you have the power to defeat him. I encourage you to pray for a hunger for the word of God like never before. It will sustain you!

Speak It:
- ♥ I cast all my burdens on God, and He sustains me!
- ♥ I have power over the enemy through the blood of Jesus!
- ♥ I take my thoughts captive and bring them under the subjection of Jesus Christ!

Day 51

"With men this is impossible; but with God all things are possible."
Matthew 19:26 (KJV)

Your new way of thinking may be new for you, but I encourage you to keep going. Renewing your mind requires a shift in what you think is normal. As you get to know your Heavenly Father for who He is and learn that you are His child, you will begin to act like Him. In addition, you will begin to walk in your faith daily. Faith is basically believing what God has said or revealed to you in His word or through prayer and walking in that revelation until it comes to pass. Now, things will still look messed up. Bills may not be paid, children may be acting up, and you may have applied for what seems like ten thousand jobs. Nonetheless, you must NOT speak against your faith! When I was purchasing my first home, I knew through God's word and through a revelation from Holy Spirit that I was to walk by faith and not by sight. It was hard to stay positive and to even think that He would bless me with a house that was built according to my own specifications.

Conversely, what I realized during that process was that God never gives up on us. Meanwhile, we constantly give up and throw Him on the backseat of our lives. It's time that you put Him first. Stop letting your thoughts get the best of you. As an alternative, take those thoughts captive that come against your destiny and your purpose. With God, you will come to know that all things are possible. Your father loves you, and He delights in the prosperity of His servants. He wants us prosperous on all levels—emotionally, mentally, physically, and financially. Walk in your new mindset moment by moment, and it will get easier every day. Your dreams and purpose are obtainable. Just watch your father leave you speechless when He pours His love on you.

Speak It:
- ♥ All things are possible with God!
- ♥ I am guided by Holy Spirit!
- ♥ My faith gets stronger every day!

Day 52

"For we walk by faith and not by sight."
2 Corinthians 5:7 (KJV)

Faith is the one thing that led me to write this devotional. It's also the one thing that will change your life, if you have faith in the right things. I used to have more faith in things and people than I had in God. I knew that my mother had my back without a doubt, and I was sure that she would come through for me. There was a time when I even relied on her Holy Spirit! I knew that she would get a "feeling" that would let her know if something was good or bad. At that time, I didn't have true faith in God. My faith became real after my first marriage continued to fail no matter what I tried to do to save it. I could only go to one person to fix my brokenness and that was God. Deciding to give up sexual activity was the first step, and it wasn't easy. However, I didn't like feeling like trash once everything was over. Relying on God when my flesh wanted to do something else, showed me that I was stronger with Him than I ever could imagine.

Changing the places that I hung in was another step for me. I literally wanted to live in the world, but I knew that I wasn't of it. Therefore, I decided to honor God and not frequent clubs and bars for fun. There was a time where I was alone, but I spent that time in my Bible. I changed my wants into doing what pleased my Father. Was it easy? Not at first. Did I make mistakes and slip up? Yes, but I knew my obedience was better than sacrificing more time that was too precious to lose. So I kept doing what would please Him no matter how I felt. In addition, I continued to be celibate. I thought when the time is right, the one who He has for me will find me, and I will be a help meet rather than a hindrance or a counterfeit.

I decided to change the way I was living in order to please Him, and it changed my outlook on life. I did not see writing a book when I started this journey, but God had a different plan. No matter what you have done or where you have been, there is a purpose for your life. It's time that you get out of the way and yield to God. Let Him heal you and mend your broken pieces so that you can share your story just like I am sharing mine with you. Faith will take you places that only God has foreseen.

Speak It:
- ♥ I walk only by faith and not by sight!
- ♥ Faith is how I please God!
- ♥ God will do exceedingly and abundantly more than I can ask, think, or imagine! The power is already within me!

Day 53

"Now the Lord is that Spirit: and where the spirit of the Lord is there is liberty."

2 Corinthians 3:17 (KJV)

As believers, we have been sent a wonderful blessing called Holy Spirit. I will keep reminding you of His presence because He is our helper, guide, intercessor, and so much more! I encourage you to get into a deep relationship with Him so that you can move into your destiny in Christ. Have you ever had an uneasy feeling like something bad was gonna happen? Maybe you have felt like you shouldn't be in a particular place or that you're not going out tonight? When you get these "feelings," it is not a coincidence nor is it that you are lucky. It's Holy Spirit giving us a warning. In order to enhance this gift from God, we must stay in communication with Him. This scripture in the Greek-Hebrew translation could be rephrased as, "Now the Lord is that Spirit and where the **gentleness** of the Lord is there is **freedom**." Have you ever noticed a calming effect when you are in church? I am at peace one hundred percent of the time when I'm at church. Even when the message is correcting me, I still have a joy in my heart. Then, my spirit is vexed again on Monday, as soon as I start driving or get to work.

We carry the spirit of the living God with us wherever we go. Did you know that? We have constant contact with our Heavenly Father. He has given us the gift of freedom 24/7! If you are even in a situation where you feel pressured, that is not from God. Anything that makes you feel less than or condemned is not God either. The main reason why we need to read the Bible is because it gives us the blueprint to life. You now know that you have freedom in the Lord. You know that His spirit is one that is gentle. So from this moment on, you will walk in faith knowing that you are free because you have the greater one on the inside of you. We please our father by walking in Faith. You walk by Faith when you know His word and His promises. I dare you to get into your Bible. Furthermore, I dare you to step into greatness knowing that Holy Spirit will guide you and nothing shall by any means harm you! Are you ready to stop letting your situations get the best of you because you feel oppressed and defeated? I know that you are! Continue opening your Bible. I promise you that God will not let you down.

Speak It:
- Where the Spirit of the Lord is, there is freedom!
- I am no longer under the curse of the law!
- I am led by Holy Spirit!

Day 54

"I [godly] wisdom, reside with prudence [good judgement, moral courage and astute common sense], And I find knowledge and discretion."
Proverbs 8:12 (AMP)

Have you ever felt like you didn't know what to do next? You probably felt like there was more to life than how you were living at that moment. However, since your life has been full of disappointments, you have decided to remain stagnant. You accept easy jobs that don't require much from you. You hide out in ministries where you don't use your real gifts. You stay silent when you have ideas that would help better people, because you think no one will listen to you. Sound familiar? If so, let's make a change today! Communicate with Holy Spirit and ask Him for wisdom on how to progress in your life. When you seek God for wisdom, good judgement, moral courage, and astute common sense will follow! What this means for you, Beloved, is that you will not have any more trouble making decisions. You will seek God for guidance, and He will be right there with the answer for you.

What you must remember is to be consistent and diligent in your approach. I've learned that God is not a genie. I cannot come to Him with three wishes, and they instantly come true! I had to seek Him and give up my fleshly desires for His will. Sometimes I felt like I was going crazy! The devil would send anything he could so that I could get discouraged or think that I didn't hear

Holy Spirit clearly. Do not fall for what you see. You are wise, Beloved, and you are filled with Godly judgement. You have to make a choice to renew you mind to the thinking of your Father. If you don't choose to go against what you see with your physical eyes, you will never succeed. Take time before you leave your home to seek God for direction and wisdom. As you make talking with God a priority, you will see a breakthrough and change in your life. Make a choice today to seek wisdom from God, and lean not unto what you can see in the natural.

Speak It:
- ♥ I seek God daily for wisdom!
- ♥ I am not moved by what I see!
- ♥ I speak to God before I make any decisions!

Day 55

"And let us not be weary in well doing for in due season we shall reap, if we faint not."
Galatians 6:9 (KJV)

On numerous occasions, I've wanted to give up. Before I really knew there was a purpose for my life, I just did whatever I wanted. Once my focus became more clear and I began to study the word more, it felt like I was an emotional mess. I was looking on social media and getting upset at the social media lives of others. I was envious because I wanted what I saw in the natural. I wanted to be married to the right man that God had for me. So when others got engaged, I would ask God, "Why isn't it my turn yet? I am celibate. I am reading your word. I am not going out partying. When is it my time?" The main theme with these questions always led back to me. I was being very selfish. I was NOT concerned with what God wanted from my life. I was only concerned with my wants. Sometimes we must check our motives. Why are you really doing what you are doing? Is it so that God can bless you, or is it because you reverence Him and you want nothing more than to please Him?

Do not misunderstand me; God will bless you in spite of yourself. On the other hand, I've learned that I cannot fool Him. No matter how much I said that marriage wasn't my focus, it was on my mind in some way. I was still affected by other people's relationship statuses. In one of my epiphanies, Holy Spirit revealed to me that what I am going through is for my destiny. The things that I sacrifice for Christ are for my good. Beloved, you should not desire what you see. Your heart's desire should be centered around what God has for you. If you are in a season where you are single, enjoy your singleness. Seek God for what He wants to do through you, and your life will change dramatically. God is not like man; He cannot lie. This verse is a guarantee for me that my well doing, my obedience, and my sacrifices will cause me to reap if I faint not. Do not give up, Beloved. Do not go back to your past. Keep looking forward to what God has for you! Your harvest is coming!

Speak It:
- ♥ My Faith is strong in Christ!
- ♥ I desire what God wants for me!
- ♥ I will NOT faint!

Day 56

> *"Now unto him that is able to do exceeding abundantly above all that we ask or think, according to the power that worketh in us."*
> Ephesians 3:20 (KJV)

This scripture is one of the most quoted scriptures in the American church, in my opinion. The only part that I never heard was the end of it. I learned from reading the full scripture that the power I need to fulfill my purpose, dreams, aspirations, and anything else is already within me! Anything that I ask for or can think of, He will exceed that. Still, the power to make those things happen is already here! It is essential that you get a clear understanding about this verse. You have Holy Spirit working inside of you. That means that you have the same power that Jesus had! The power of Holy Spirit operates in and through you. Have you ever wondered why things aren't changing in your life? It may be because you have not tapped into the source of your abundance!

Where is your focus? Is it on circumstance or is it on Christ? You may be able to quote this scripture, but it does you no good if you do not believe it! Satan has already been defeated thousands of years ago. He knows it; you just have to wrap your mind around your victory. When you accepted Christ as your savior, your sins were erased, you were accepted into the Beloved, and Satan was put in his place under your feet. You have power to trample over all the power of the enemy, and NOTHING will harm you! It's time for you to possess your exceeding and abundant power, Beloved. Don't let another day go by with you speaking words of defeat. Speak life over yourself and every situation that tries to get your focus off God. You are a winner, and the POWER is already in you! It's time to go to work!

Speak It:
- ♥ God's blessings exceed anything I have dreamed!
- ♥ The power to overcome is already within me!
- ♥ I walk in my God-given power!

Day 57

"After you have suffered for a little while, the God of all grace [who imparts His blessing and favor], who called you to His own eternal glory in Christ, will Himself complete, confirm, strengthen, and establish you [making you what you ought to be]."

1 Peter 5:10 (AMP)

Have you made decisions without consulting with the One who knows the plans that He has for your life? If so, you are not alone. When I tried to plan my life without the input of God, every attempt was a failure and it took me off the course He had for my life. In making my own plans, I suffered for what seemed like forever. When we choose to live life based on what we think we want, there will be some suffering. Until we decide to die to ourselves, we will continue to live an unfulfilled life. It's time to live for Him! This scripture lets you know that God imparts blessings and favor towards you. He has called you into greatness in Christ. The BEST part is that He will complete you, confirm you, and make you what you OUGHT to be!

He will grace you, Beloved! The confirmation that you need is in Christ. The strength that you need to push forward is in Christ. The thing that always seems to be missing, the reason you can't sleep at night, the spot that no man can fill, Christ is the One who fills that spot! Stop suffering, and seek Him. All you have to do is ask. It's time to be diligent about the things of Christ and become unshakeable in your faith. You may have stopped reading this devotional or your Bible for a while, but it does not matter. Do not let the enemy of your soul continue to condemn you. God is merciful, and He is waiting for you to come to Him so that He can transform you in Him. You are worthy of His love, and it is time for you to take action! You are His, and nothing will ever change how much He loves you!

Speak It:
- ♥ God imparts blessings and favor towards me!
- ♥ I am complete in Christ!
- ♥ I am established in Christ!

Day 58

"But without faith it is impossible to [walk with God and] please Him, for whoever comes [near] to God must [necessarily] believe that God exists and that He rewards those who [earnestly and diligently] seek Him."
Hebrews 11:6 (AMP)

I have mentioned this before, and it is worth repeating every time. You MUST have a confident expectation towards Christ. You MUST believe with everything in you that He will do EVERYTHING the word of God says. Without it, it is impossible to please Him. If you have made it this far through the devotional, I pray that you believe that God exists. One thing that I have overcome is being a quitter. I would get focused for two seconds on God, and then run when I thought "love" had found me. I never took the time to learn God's love for me. Therefore, every time this "love" came along, I ran towards it and left God on the shelf. The most important thing about this journey has been being consistent. There have been times when I did not want to write, and times when I didn't feel like God was with me. There were also times when I thought that He wasn't working fast enough, but I had to check myself. God had been patiently and earnestly waiting for me to seek HIM. Every time I decided that He wasn't important, He still waited for me. He protected, provided, and professed His love for me every time my family's needs were met.

Do not be fooled by what you see around you. It's very important for you to make a conscientious effort to seek

God. Continue to read your Bible when the bills are late. Soon, you will be able to pay them with money left over. Pray to Him when you don't feel like praying. Those feelings are temporary. Just know that your natural body will feel refreshed once you have found Him. He has every answer that you are looking for, Beloved. When you continue to seek Him, be aware of your changing identity. You will be more confident. You will change the way you act, think, and speak. Do NOT let the enemy tell you that you are not worth it! He is a liar. God will reward you! Your efforts are not in vain. He hears every cry and sees everything you are turning down for His sake. The rewards will overtake you, and you will not have room to store them! Get ready to receive Christ, and tell the world your testimony!

Speak It:
- ♥ God rewards me for my diligence!
- ♥ I have confident expectations in Christ!
- ♥ Overflow is already mine!

Day 59

> *"But you shall remember [with profound respect] the L*ORD *your God, for it is He who is giving you power to make wealth, that He may confirm His covenant which He swore (solemnly promised) to your fathers, as it is this day."*
> Deuteronomy 8:18 (AMP)

How are you doing in the finance department? If your money is stable, and you are not living paycheck to paycheck, I would high-five you if we were next to each other. ☺ On the other hand, if you are living paycheck to paycheck, I have some good news for you! It will NOT always be like that. If you are a single mother, a woman who has been divorced and you are making adjustments, or maybe you just do not make enough money, know that God never intended for you to live in lack. I lived that way for a long time, and I was very unhappy. I was easily frustrated, and the words that came out of my mouth stalled my harvest. I would say things like, "It's never enough! I am tired of living paycheck to paycheck!" I was speaking against what the word of God says, especially since I was a tither. Whatever your situation is know that God gives you the power to get wealth.

What this meant for me was that once I sought Him and His ways, I became more diligent in how I spent money and what I said. This new way of living gave me the desire to stop living in lack. As I moved forward into my purpose, God revealed multiple streams of income. One thing I will mention is that if I didn't renew my mind to my identity in Christ, I would have not been able to step out in faith and be bold enough to do the things that I used to be afraid to do. You are BOLD in Christ, Beloved! You have a covenant with God, and He is faithful to perform it! Remember that when you think that you cannot go on or when you are walking by sight instead of faith. Continue to please your Father with what comes out of your mouth! Declare and decree financial stability, and it will be added unto you! Let God use you for His kingdom, and you will be wealthy on every level!

Speak It:
- God gives me the power to get wealth!
- I am diligent with my income!
- I am financially stable!

Day 60

"I will give thanks and praise to You, for I am fearfully and wonderfully made; Wonderful are Your works, And my soul knows it very well."
Psalms 139:14 (AMP)

    I never thought that I was good enough. Even after losing weight, having boyfriends, being married, and becoming a Registered Nurse, I still didn't think I was good enough. It wasn't until I was single, which was very shocking for me, that I realized I was fearless and wonderful! You already know that relationships were my desire. I felt they would make me whole. I also realized I had a relationship problem with women. I would get upset and shut down if my girls didn't reach out to me at the same capacity as I did them. I was very needy for attention. I didn't want anyone to leave me. Do you have some of these characteristics? If you do, you can release that fear to Christ. If you feel yourself regressing even for a split second, acknowledge that you feel that way, and give it right to Him. I do so continually until I am completely fearless.
    I don't hold on to insecurities anymore. I don't hold on to fear. I know that my God will never leave me or forsake me. I also know from meditating on this scripture that whatever God makes is wonderful, and He made me in His image! I don't have to have long hair, weigh a certain amount, or talk a certain way to be loved or to make someone stay. I am Geneva, and that is enough for my Father. I thank God for being merciful and giving us

Holy Spirit who comforts us. He also made you, Beloved. It's time for you to see yourself as wonderful. You are marvelous, lovely, and awesome! Regardless of whatever someone has said in your past, give those negative things to God. During this process of renewal, you will continue to rid yourself of all negative things and memories. It will become easier to cast down those thoughts. Just keep going! Do NOT quit! Praise God even when you don't feel like it! That is an action of faith, and that pleases your Father! Let your soul rest and know that YOU ARE ENOUGH!

Speak It:
- ♥ I am fearfully and wonderfully made!
- ♥ I am enough in Christ!
- ♥ My soul finds rest in God!

Day 61

> *"For whoever finds me (Wisdom) finds life and obtains favor and grace from the LORD."*
> Proverbs 8:35 (AMP)

I like to call the book of Proverbs, the Wisdom Book. In every chapter, it gives specific instructions on how to live a life for Christ. It explains what to do and what not to do. Wisdom is synonymous with intelligence, common sense, and good judgement. When we seek God through His word, we receive knowledge/wisdom about how we should live our lives. When we apply this knowledge, we live for Him and not for self. This produces faith in Christ, and we find our life in Him. When I started living my life based on what He wanted, I received blessings that other people would call luck because no one else received that favor.

When you decide to walk in the wisdom of Christ, people will begin to notice that everything that you say comes to pass. If you call yourself blessed, you will be blessed. Call your children and family prosperous, and they will be prosperous. Confess that you have zero student loan debt, and you WILL have zero student loan debt. Wisdom is one of the most important traits that you should seek after, Beloved. When you have this knowledge pertaining to God's word, you will find the life you have been missing! The favor of God will surround you like a shield. Everywhere you look, blessings will be there. Seek Him, and you will retain His wisdom. You will be filled with insight that other people do not have—

insight on how you should live, move, and who you should befriend or even date. Your father wants to bless you! Continue to search for Him; knock and He will answer. Seek and you will find Him. Be diligent in following His commands, and you'll always have an expectant mindset because you know He will NEVER let you down!

Speak It:
- ♥ I am filled with Wisdom!
- ♥ My life is filled with Purpose!
- ♥ Favor and Grace surrounds me!

Day 62

"And I will restore to you the years that the locust hath eaten, the cankerworm, and the caterpillar, and the palmerworm, my great army which I sent among you."

Joel 2:25 (KJV)

    I pray that as you've been reading this devotional and seeking God, your view about yourself has changed. I know there may be some days when you feel like you are being attacked. Guess what? That is a good thing! Whenever you feel like you are being attacked, praise God! Whenever we praise God during adversity, it confuses the enemy! You've been consistent in seeking God, and He sees your efforts. He will continue to be your rewarder when you seek Him. I am reminding you that you are His Beloved because the enemy may try to make you think that you do not deserve to be blessed. He may try to make you think you aren't worthy, BUT YOU ARE! No matter what you've done, where you were two weeks ago, or who you may have hurt, you are STILL His child. Whatever has been stolen, let go, or you decided you didn't deserve WILL be restored to you!

    God can make things happen instantly! He can restore your mind, heart, marriage, and family! Beloved, keep going! Keep seeking! Whatever He has instructed you to do, get it done! Obedience opens doors of provision! I am a witness of this. This devotional is a product of obedience. The enemy tried several times to make me think I wasn't good enough to be an author. He told me I wasn't a preacher or teacher, so I shouldn't be writing this. One thing he did not realize is that he couldn't keep me in condemnation forever! What he doesn't know is that you are realizing that you can defeat him! You are overcoming all the lies that he has ever told you, and you are RESTORED in Jesus' name. Notice that I am already speaking restoration. Do not wait until you see it. Speak it before you see it, and it will manifest in your life! You are restored, Beloved! I think it's time that you praise God!

Speak It:
- ♥ God has restored every area of my life!
- ♥ My identity is established in Christ!
- ♥ I wait with confident expectation!

Day 63

> *"And be not conformed to this world: but be ye transformed by the renewing of your mind, that ye may prove what is that good, and acceptable, and perfect, will of God."*
>
> Romans 12:2 (KJV)

I keep stressing the importance of seeking God. I know it may seem a bit redundant, but an intimate one-on-one relationship is essential for your transformation. I know that because I wasn't serious about my walk with God in the beginning. As a result, it took me longer to understand my identity in Him. There is no way to be like the world and live for Christ. One will trump the other. If you don't know who you are in Christ, the world will snatch you back every time. You can NOT conform to this world! Beloved, I encourage you with everything in me to go hard after God. As you keep reading His word, attending church, confessing, and praying you will be transformed! Your mind will be renewed daily to who you really are. That is why it is essential that you do not go a day without Him.

If you spend time reading devotionals or your Bible, these two things done continually with prayer will give you a solid foundation. You will not have any space for the enemy to creep in and plant seeds of confusion or discord in your life. When we are transformed, we show the world that God is still alive. Furthermore, we show the world that He is a forgiving God. He still loves us no matter what we've done! His will is good, acceptable, and perfect. His plan is perfect just for you, Beloved. He sees you, and He is pleased with what you have done so far for His kingdom and what you will continue to do to affect the world! Do not think that you are weird or the only one who is living for God, because you are NOT! I pray that God leads you to strong Christian women who will be able to pray with you and lift you up with the word of God. Do not change to fit in with others! Let them see your light and want to follow you because of the Christ they see in you! It's time for you to show the world who your savior is!

Speak It:
- ♥ I am transformed in Christ!
- ♥ My mind is renewed in Christ!
- ♥ I am blessed with Kingdom connections!

Day 64

"A capable, intelligent, and virtuous woman- who is he who can find her? She is far more precious than jewels and her value is far above rubies or pearls."
Proverbs 31:10 (AMP)

Beloved, do you know that you are a virtuous woman? You are a woman of excellence! You are a woman who knows who she is in Christ and will NOT let anyone or anything devalue her! It took me a while to understand my value. It's easy to say, "I know my worth! I'm not accepting anything or anyone less than what I deserve." However, when you find yourself accepting any man that comes your way and thinking that you can change him or that he will love you to a place where you will be fulfilled, then you still DON'T see yourself as you should. I thought that a man could fill my empty spots. I was wrong, and I learned the hard way. Even though I was intelligent and capable of taking care of myself, I was emotionally bruised. Thank God for being a healer!

No matter where you are emotionally, there is potential for healing. Your broken pieces can be mended with God continually showing His love for you. You are capable of a God kind of love, but you must first love HIM. You are more precious to Him than you can imagine. I couldn't imagine His love for me when I was seeking it from other men, but He waited for me to come back. He wanted me to come to Him and let him mold me into the virtuous woman that I know you can be also! It is my prayer that as you have read this devotional, your relationship with Him has shown you things that you would have never known. I pray that He has shown you which areas need healing and that you are giving Him those hurts and issues daily. You are amazing, Beloved! You are valuable, and I am amazed at your strength! You are an emotional miracle!

Speak It:
- ♥ I am a virtuous woman!
- ♥ I am whole in Christ!
- ♥ I know my worth!

Day 65

"Beloved, I pray that you may prosper in every way and [that your body] may keep well, even as [I know] your soul keeps well and prospers."

3 John 1:2 (AMP)

I thank God for everything that I thought was a battle in my life. I thank God for letting me be overweight and for my two children. Moreover, I thank God that He gives us free will. Everything that I have been through has brought me to a place where I could heal someone else. What I thought would break me, brought me closer to God and showed me that I am His Beloved. This scripture is my prayer for you. I pray that these sixty-five scriptures have helped you get closer to Christ. I pray that your spirit is being transformed and renewed and that you are prospering daily.

These scriptures are continually replaying in my mind so that I NEVER forget who I am! Never forget that you deserve a life filled with love, joy, and peace. Remember that you are in this world, but you are not of it! You have the right to live a purpose-filled life. Someone needs to hear your story! You have completed a journey during these sixty-five days. You are an overcomer! Your soul is well, and you are prosperous in Christ. Nothing can hold you back, because the power to succeed is already within you! Step out in faith and live life to the fullest. I can't wait to hear your testimony! Know that I am forever grateful that you took this journey with me and that you decided to walk in Faith and NOT by sight!

YOU ARE HIS BELOVED!

Speak It:
- ♥ God is birthing new ideas in me!
- ♥ I will go where God tells me!
- ♥ I will say what God instructs me to say!

Speak It

- God equips me with EVERYTHING that I need to succeed!
- I will always be in top condition!
- I will complete every task that is set before me!
- My true identity is established in Christ!
- God loved me before the foundations of the earth!
- God has mended my broken heart and damaged areas!
- I will not let my past hinder me from moving into my future!
- I am made alive in Christ!
- I accept God's love towards me!
- God is with me, and I am healed!
- God is my restorer!
- I seek God daily!
- I trust God!
- I am preserved by God!
- I cast all my cares on God!
- I am a new creature in Christ!
- I speak only what the word of God says that I am!
- I am blessed!
- I am steadfast and immovable, always abounding in the Lord!
- My identity is defined in Christ!
- I always complete every task that I start!
- In peace, I lay down and sleep at night!
- I am not worried about anything, because my trust is in God!
- God provides me with peace that surpasses all my understanding!

- ♥ I hear from God clearly!
- ♥ God is the planner of my life!
- ♥ I live out my purpose in God!
- ♥ I acknowledge God in all my ways!
- ♥ I am not of this world!
- ♥ I am victorious!
- ♥ I walk after the Spirit and not the Flesh!
- ♥ There is now no condemnation, because I am in Christ Jesus!
- ♥ I include God in every area of my life!
- ♥ God hears my heartfelt fervent prayers!
- ♥ God's word does not return void!
- ♥ I meditate on the word day and night!
- ♥ God knows my expected end!
- ♥ The joy of the Lord is my strength!
- ♥ I bring into captivity every thought to the obedience of Christ!
- ♥ I walk by Faith and not by sight!
- ♥ The Lord causes me to triumph!
- ♥ In my weakness, I am made strong through Christ!
- ♥ I am steadfast and immovable!
- ♥ My faith brings forth patience!
- ♥ I trust God to lead me!
- ♥ I am steadfast!
- ♥ I am stable-minded!
- ♥ I am patient!
- ♥ I am complete and whole in God!
- ♥ I will pass this test!
- ♥ I am slow to speak, slow to wrath, and swift to hear!
- ♥ The Lord fights all my battles!
- ♥ I walk in love daily!
- ♥ I fear NOTHING!
- ♥ I have unshakeable faith!
- ♥ I walk by faith!

- I have a supernatural extension of benefits!
- I have kingdom relationships!
- I only listen to wise counsel!
- I overflow with wisdom!
- I am a chose generation!
- I am royalty!
- I am an heir according to the promise!
- I will receive a double portion for my shame!
- I have everlasting joy!
- The joy of the Lord gives me strength!
- I have the spirit of a finisher!
- I have confidence in God!
- I can trample over scorpions, serpents, and over all the power of the enemy, and NOTHING shall harm me!
- I am led by Holy Spirit!
- I will accomplish all of my goals!
- I set my thoughts on things above and not on things of this world!
- I wait with confidence for the things that God has for me!
- I desire His will for my life!
- I am an overcomer!
- I have peace in every situation!
- I speak life over myself and not death!
- I will bless the Lord, and His praises shall continually be in my mouth!
- I speak words of life!
- I can decree a desire, and it will be established unto me!
- I am blessed and highly favored!
- I confess the name of Jesus before men!
- I will stand firm on my faith in Christ!
- I am bold in Christ!
- All things work together for my good!
- I am called according to God's purpose!

- ♥ I have the power to complete my God-given assignments!
- ♥ Nothing can separate me from the love of God!
- ♥ I am equipped with everything that I need in Christ!
- ♥ Patience is having her perfect work!
- ♥ I will love God with all my heart, soul, mind, and strength!
- ♥ God has already placed everything I need within me!
- ♥ I walk by faith and not by sight!
- ♥ I give all of my broken pieces to Christ!
- ♥ Through Christ, I am made new!
- ♥ My heart is made new in Christ!
- ♥ I trust in the Lord with all my heart!
- ♥ I acknowledge the Lord first, and He directs my path!
- ♥ I have patience to wait on an answer from God!
- ♥ When I am weak, God's grace is sufficient and makes me strong!
- ♥ I am an overcomer!
- ♥ I let God lead me into my purpose and destiny!
- ♥ God knows the plans that He has for me—thoughts of peace and not of evil!
- ♥ I will openly accept God's love!
- ♥ I am spotless and blameless in His sight!
- ♥ I speak with God's wisdom!
- ♥ I only speak faith-filled words!
- ♥ Greater is He that is in me than he that is in this world!
- ♥ I walk in the Spirit and not in the flesh!
- ♥ Holy Spirit is my helper and my guide!
- ♥ I have a listening ear to Holy Spirit!
- ♥ God will provide me with a way of escape!
- ♥ I am victorious in Christ!
- ♥ Nothing shall harm me by any means!

- ♥ I delight myself in the Lord daily!
- ♥ I seek after Christ with my whole heart!
- ♥ I have faith that pleases God!
- ♥ I seek first the kingdom of God!
- ♥ I consult with God before anyone else!
- ♥ I do not worry about anything!
- ♥ God will never leave me nor forsake me!
- ♥ I do not covet the things of others!
- ♥ What God has for _____ (Insert Name) is for _____ (Insert Name).
- ♥ I am chosen by God!
- ♥ I am of a royal priesthood!
- ♥ I belong exclusively to Christ!
- ♥ I am the head and not the tail!
- ♥ I am above only and not beneath!
- ♥ I am a follower of God's commandments!
- ♥ I am the daughter of the Most High God!
- ♥ I give myself to God!
- ♥ I am His beloved!
- ♥ I choose life!
- ♥ I follow the straight path in Christ Jesus!
- ♥ I seek God and know that He is my rewarder!
- ♥ I am a doer of the Word of God!
- ♥ In Christ, I have a solid foundation!
- ♥ I listen and follow Christ's instructions!
- ♥ I cast all my anxieties on God!
- ♥ I find sweet rest in His presence!
- ♥ I have peace that surpasses my understanding!
- ♥ I walk after the Spirit and not the flesh!
- ♥ My Spirit is getting stronger each day!
- ♥ I sacrifice my will for the will of God!
- ♥ If God be for me, no one can be against me!
- ♥ I speak faith-filled words!
- ♥ I will continue to walk by Faith and not by sight!
- ♥ I have mountain moving Faith!

- Nothing is impossible with Christ!
- I speak to my mountains, and they are removed!
- I am a tither, and God will pour out a blessing so big that I will not have room enough to store it!
- I am a tither, and God rebukes the devourer for my sake!
- I am a cheerful giver!
- I cast all my burdens on God, and He sustains me!
- I have power over the enemy through the blood of Jesus!
- I take my thoughts captive and bring them under the subjection of Jesus Christ!
- All things are possible with God!
- I am guided by Holy Spirit!
- My faith gets stronger every day!
- I walk only by faith and not by sight!
- Faith is how I please God!
- God will do exceedingly and abundantly more than I can ask, think, or imagine! The power is already within me!
- Where the Spirit of the Lord is, there is freedom!
- I am no longer under the curse of the law!
- I am led by Holy Spirit!
- I seek God daily for wisdom!
- I am not moved by what I see!
- I speak to God before I make any decisions!
- My Faith is strong in Christ!
- I desire what God wants for me!
- I will NOT faint!
- God's blessings exceed anything I have dreamed!
- The power to overcome is already within me!
- I walk in my God-given power!
- God imparts blessings and favor towards me!
- I am complete in Christ!
- I am established in Christ!

- ♥ God rewards me for my diligence!
- ♥ I have confident expectations in Christ!
- ♥ Overflow is already mine!
- ♥ God gives me the power to get wealth!
- ♥ I am diligent with my income!
- ♥ I am financially stable!
- ♥ I am fearfully and wonderfully made!
- ♥ I am enough in Christ!
- ♥ My soul finds rest in God!
- ♥ I am filled with Wisdom!
- ♥ My life is filled with Purpose!
- ♥ Favor and Grace surrounds me!
- ♥ God has restored every area of my life!
- ♥ My identity is established in Christ!
- ♥ I wait with confident expectation!
- ♥ I am transformed in Christ!
- ♥ My mind is renewed in Christ!
- ♥ I am blessed with Kingdom connections!
- ♥ I am a virtuous woman!
- ♥ I am whole in Christ!
- ♥ I know my worth!
- ♥ God is birthing new ideas in me!
- ♥ I will go where God tells me!
- ♥ I will say what God instructs me to say!
- ♥ I am lead by Christ!
- ♥ I surrender to the will of Christ for my life!
- ♥ I have a Kingdom mindset!

If you enjoyed this book, you may also enjoy His Beloved Workbook.

About the Author

Geneva Jewel is a Christian Life Coach, entrepreneur, and philanthropist. Geneva is a nurse by trade, but she now spends her time nursing her clients' emotional health. Geneva Jewel's signature program *Emotional Bootcamp (EBC)* was created to help women discover who they are in Christ, transform their thinking, and develop strategies to overcome their emotions to ultimately change their lives.

Geneva's mission is for her clients to Write it, Speak it, See it! She believes what you speak *F.R.A.M.E.*'s your life: **F**aith is our **R**eality through **A**ffirmations, **M**editation, and great **E**xpectation!

Geneva enjoys spending time with family and friends, reading, and traveling. Geneva lives in Delaware with her husband, Garth, and two children.

To learn more about books by Geneva Jewel or subscribe to her motivational e-newsletter visit her website at www.GenevaJewel.com.

www.ingramcontent.com/pod-product-compliance
Lightning Source LLC
Chambersburg PA
CBHW031149160426
43193CB00008B/299